HOUSING ISSUES, LAWS AND PROGRAMS

# QUALIFIED MORTGAGES

## ELEMENTS AND POTENTIAL EFFECTS

# HOUSING ISSUES, LAWS AND PROGRAMS

Additional books in this series can be found on Nova's website under the Series tab.

Additional e-books in this series can be found on Nova's website under the e-book tab.

HOUSING ISSUES, LAWS AND PROGRAMS

# QUALIFIED MORTGAGES

## ELEMENTS AND POTENTIAL EFFECTS

BRENDA MILLS
EDITOR

nova
publishers
*New York*

**Library of Congress Cataloging-in-Publication Data**

ISBN: 978-1-63484-559-5

*Published by Nova Science Publishers, Inc. † New York*

# Contents

# PREFACE

During the years preceding the mortgage crisis, too many mortgages were made to consumers without regard to the consumers' ability to repay the loans. Loose underwriting practices by some creditors – including failure to verify consumers' income or debts and qualifying consumers for mortgages based on "teaser" interest rates after which monthly payments would jump to unaffordable levels – contributed to a mortgage crisis that led to the nation's most serious recession since the Great Depression. Amid concerns that risky mortgage products and poor underwriting standards contributed to the recent housing crisis, Congress included mortgage reform provisions (qualified mortgage (QM) and qualified residential mortgage (QRM)) in the Dodd-Frank Wall Street Reform and Consumer Protection Act. The Consumer Financial Protection Bureau's (CFPB) regulations establishing standards for QM loans became effective in January 2014. More recently, six agencies jointly issued the final QRM rule that will become effective in December 2015. This book discusses views on the expected effects of the QM and QRM regulations, and examines the extent of agency planning for reviewing the regulations' effects, among its objectives.

In: Qualified Mortgages
Editor: Brenda Mills
ISBN: 978-1-63484-559-5


*Chapter 1*

# MORTGAGE REFORMS: ACTIONS NEEDED TO HELP ASSESS EFFECTS OF NEW REGULATIONS*

***United States Government Accountability Office***

## WHY GAO DID THIS STUDY

Amid concerns that risky mortgage products and poor underwriting standards contributed to the recent housing crisis, Congress included mortgage reform provisions (QM and QRM) in the Dodd-Frank Wall Street Reform and Consumer Protection Act. CFPB's regulations establishing standards for QM loans became effective in January 2014. More recently, six agencies jointly issued the final QRM rule that will become effective in December 2015. GAO was asked to review possible effects of these regulations. This report (1) discusses views on the expected effects of the QM and QRM regulations, and (2) examines the extent of agency planning for reviewing the regulations' effects, among its objectives. GAO's methodologies included identifying and reviewing academic, industry, and federal agency analyses on the expected effects of the regulations. GAO also reviewed federal guidance on retrospective reviews and interviewed agency officials to assess agency efforts to examine the effects of the QM and QRM regulations.

* This is an edited, reformatted and augmented version of the United States Government Accountability Office publication, GAO-15-185, dated June 2015.

## What GAO Recommends

CFPB, HUD, and the six agencies responsible for the QRM regulations should complete plans to review the QM and QRM regulations, including identifying specific metrics, baselines, and analytical methods. CFPB, HUD, and one QRM agency—the Federal Deposit Insurance Corporation—concurred or agreed with the recommendations. The other QRM agencies did not explicitly agree with the recommendations, but outlined ongoing efforts to plan their reviews.

## What GAO Found

Federal agency officials, market participants, and observers estimated that the qualified mortgage (QM) and qualified residential mortgage (QRM) regulations would have limited initial effects because most loans originated in recent years largely conformed with QM criteria.

- The QM regulations, which address lenders' responsibilities to determine a borrower's ability to repay a loan, set forth standards that include prohibitions on risky loan features (such as interest-only or balloon payments) and limits on points and fees. Lenders that originate QM loans receive certain liability protections.
- Securities collateralized exclusively by residential mortgages that are "qualified residential mortgages" are exempt from risk-retention requirements. The QRM regulations align the QRM definition with QM; thus, securities collateralized solely by QM loans are not subject to risk-retention requirements.

The analyses GAO reviewed estimated limited effects on the availability of mortgages for most borrowers and that any cost increases (for borrowers, lenders, and investors) would mostly stem from litigation and compliance issues. According to agency officials and observers, the QRM regulations were unlikely to have a significant initial effect on the availability or securitization of mortgages in the current market, largely because the majority of loans originated were expected to be QM loans. However, questions remain about the size and viability of the secondary market for non-QRM-backed securities.

Agencies have begun planning their reviews of the QM and QRM regulations (due January and commencing December 2019, respectively); however, these efforts have not included elements important for conducting effective retrospective reviews. Federal guidance encourages agencies to preplan their retrospective reviews and carefully consider how best to promote empirical testing of the effects of rules. To varying degrees, the relevant agencies have identified outcomes to examine, potential data sources, and analytical methods. But existing data lack important information relevant to the regulations (such as loan performance or borrower debt to income) and planned data enhancements may not be available before agencies start the reviews. The Bureau of Consumer Financial Protection (CFPB) has proposed expanding Home Mortgage Disclosure Act data reporting requirements, but the earliest that the enhanced data will be available is 2017. Similarly, the Department of Housing and Urban Development (HUD) identified how it intends to examine its QM regulations and some potential data sources but has yet to determine how it would measure the effects of these regulations, including metrics, baselines, and analytical methods. Agencies also have not specified how they will conduct their reviews, including determining which data and analytical methods to use. Finalizing plans to retrospectively review the mortgage regulations will position the agencies to better measure the effects of the QM and QRM regulations and identify any unintended consequences. Additionally, the agencies could better understand data limitations and methodological challenges and have sufficient time to develop methods to deal with these limitations and challenges.

## ABBREVIATIONS

| | |
|---|---|
| ARM | adjustable-rate mortgage |
| ATR/QM | Ability-to-Repay and Qualified Mortgage Standards |
| CFPB | Consumer Financial Protection Bureau |
| Dodd-Frank Act | Dodd-Frank Wall Street Reform and Consumer Protection Act |
| FDIC | Federal Deposit Insurance Corporation |
| Federal Reserve | Board of Governors of the Federal Reserve System |
| FHA | Federal Housing Administration |
| FHFA | Federal Housing Finance Agency |
| HMDA | Home Mortgage Disclosure Act |

| | |
|---|---|
| HUD | Department of Housing and Urban Development |
| OCC | Office of the Comptroller of the Currency |
| OMB | Office of Management and Budget |
| QM | qualified mortgage |
| QRM | qualified residential mortgage |
| SEC | Securities and Exchange Commission |
| TILA | Truth in Lending Act |
| VA | Department of Veterans Affairs |

***

June 25, 2015

The Honorable Randy Neugebauer
Chairman
Subcommittee on Financial Institutions and Consumer Credit
Committee on Financial Services
House of Representatives

The Honorable Sean Duffy
Chairman
Subcommittee on Oversight and Investigations
Committee on Financial Services
House of Representatives

The Honorable Patrick McHenry
Vice-Chairman
Committee on Financial Services
House of Representatives

The Honorable Shelly Moore Capito
United States Senate

The foreclosure crisis was fueled in part by the proliferation in the early to mid-2000s of risky mortgage products and loosened underwriting standards that have come to be associated with unusually high loan losses. One financial analytics firm estimated that the realized losses associated with defaulted residential mortgages totaled about $920 billion from 2006 through 2012.[1]

These products included mortgages with interest rates that increased sharply after a few years, did not require a down payment or full documentation of income, or allowed borrowers to defer principal and interest payments, increasing their indebtedness over time. During this period, securitization practices included bundling high- risk mortgages into residential mortgage-backed securities. As demand for the securities grew, lenders and securitizers (also known as sponsors) increasingly were compensated based on loan volume rather than loan quality, contributing to a decline in underwriting standards.

Congress passed the Dodd-Frank Wall Street Reform and Consumer Protection Act (Dodd-Frank Act) in 2010 to help prevent a recurrence of such problems in the mortgage market, among other things.[2] Section 1411 of the Dodd-Frank Act generally requires lenders to make a reasonable and good faith determination of a consumer's ability to repay a residential mortgage loan. According to section 1412 of the Dodd-Frank Act, a lender is presumed to have satisfied the ability-to-repay requirement and receives certain protection from liability when it originates a "qualified mortgage" (QM). To implement the ability-to-repay and QM provisions of the Dodd-Frank Act, the Bureau of Consumer Financial Protection (known as CFPB) issued a final rule amending Regulation Z, which implements the Truth in Lending Act (TILA).[3] Regulation Z already had a prohibition against lenders making "higher-priced" mortgage loans without regard to a consumer's ability to repay the loan. The final rule—Ability-to-Repay and Qualified Mortgage Standards (ATR/QM) under the Truth in Lending Act (Regulation Z), effective in January 10, 2014—applies expanded ability-to-repay considerations to most residential mortgage loans and defines QM. The Dodd-Frank Act also required the Department of Housing and Urban Development (HUD), Department of Veterans Affairs (VA), Department of Agriculture (USDA), and USDA Rural Housing Service to issue rules to implement the QM provisions. (For the purposes of this report, we define "QM regulations" as the segments of the final rules that implement section 1412 of the Dodd- Frank Act.) The QM regulations are intended to help protect consumers from risky types of mortgages while ensuring access to credit.

The Dodd-Frank Act also requires securitizers to retain a financial exposure of no less than 5 percent of the credit risk of any asset that they, through the issuance of asset-backed securities, transfer to a third party (risk retention). The Dodd-Frank Act creates an exception to this requirement if a mortgage-backed security is collateralized exclusively by residential mortgages that meet a separate set of criteria (to be defined by regulators) that are associated with a lower risk of default.[4] Securitized mortgages that meet these criteria are referred to as "qualified residential mortgages" (QRM). The risk-retention provision is designed to protect investors from losses and improve financial stability. To implement the risk-retention requirements of the Dodd Frank Act, six agencies jointly issued a final rule—Credit Risk Retention—in December 2014 that, among other things, defines QRM as equivalent to QM.[5] The rule will be effective for residential mortgage-backed securities in December 2015 and other asset-backed securities in December 2016. (For the purposes of this report, we use "QRM regulations" to refer to the provisions of the risk-retention rule that define QRM.)

A key challenge in implementing the QM provisions of the Dodd-Frank Act was balancing the goal of protecting borrowers with the goal of maintaining broad access to mortgage credit. Similarly, a key challenge in implementing the QRM provisions of the Dodd-Frank Act was balancing the goal of protecting investors with preserving access to affordable mortgage credit. Members of Congress and others have expressed concerns that the regulations implementing these provisions could affect the cost, availability, origination, and securitization of residential mortgages.

This report (1) describes selected trends in the origination and securitization of residential mortgages in 2000–2014; (2) discusses views on the expected effects of the QM and QRM regulations on the residential mortgage market; and (3) examines the extent to which federal agencies have plans in place to monitor and assess the effects of the QM and QRM regulations on the residential mortgage market.

To describe residential mortgage trends in 2000–2014, we selected key mortgage market indicators, including mortgage originations, interest rates, mortgage foreclosure and default rates, and mortgage-backed security issuances. We used mortgage data from federal and mortgage industry sources, including Inside Mortgage Finance, CoreLogic LLC, Freddie Mac, Mortgage Bankers Association, and the National Bureau of Economic Research. We reviewed information on the data sources, interviewed knowledgeable officials about data accuracy, and reviewed data quality information and corroborating information. We determined these data to be sufficiently reliable for our purposes.

To examine the expected effects of the QM and QRM regulations on the residential mortgage market, we identified and reviewed economic analyses that examined the potential effects.[6] We identified estimates of the regulations' effects and believe the analyses are generally reliable for our purposes. To perform a consistent review of these studies, we used a structured instrument that identified important characteristics for high- quality analyses. We reviewed *Federal Register* releases and comment letters associated with the promulgation of the regulations. We interviewed agency officials, stakeholders, and others on their views of the potential effects of the regulations. Specifically, we interviewed officials from CFPB, HUD, Department of the Treasury's Office of Financial Research, Federal Deposit Insurance Corporation (FDIC), Federal Housing Finance Agency (FHFA), Board of Governors of the Federal Reserve System (Federal Reserve), Financial Stability Oversight Council, Office of the Comptroller of the Currency (OCC), and Securities and Exchange Commission (SEC). We interviewed a range of groups representing mortgage market participants, including mortgage lenders, securitizers, investors, and consumers and representatives of credit rating agencies. We chose these groups and individuals because they had a range of views.

To examine the extent to which federal agencies have plans to monitor and assess the effects of the QM and QRM regulations, we identified and reviewed requirements and guidance for monitoring and assessing regulations. Specifically, we reviewed provisions of the Dodd-Frank Act that require CFPB to assess its significant rules and report on its assessment, Executive Orders related to retrospective reviews, and associated Office of Management and Budget (OMB) memorandums. We focused on the retrospective review activities of CFPB and the six agencies responsible for the QRM regulations—FDIC, FHFA, Federal Reserve, HUD, OCC, and SEC. We reviewed *Federal Register* releases and other agency documents pertaining to retrospective reviews. We interviewed agency officials from the seven agencies listed earlier about their plans to retrospectively review the QM and QRM regulations. See appendix I for a detailed description of our scope and methodology.

We conducted this performance audit from November 2013 to June 2015 in accordance with generally accepted government auditing standards. Those standards require that we plan and perform the audit to obtain sufficient, appropriate evidence to provide a reasonable basis for our findings and conclusions based on our audit objectives. We believe that the evidence obtained provides a reasonable basis for our findings and conclusions based on our audit objectives.

# BACKGROUND

## Residential Mortgage Categories and Securitization

Two types of residential mortgage loans are common: fixed-rate mortgages, which have interest rates that do not change over the entire term of the loans, and adjustable-rate mortgages (ARM), which have interest rates that change periodically based on changes in a specified index.

Residential mortgages also fall into several loosely defined categories:

- Prime mortgages are made to borrowers with strong credit histories and provide the most attractive interest rates and loan terms;
- Near-prime mortgages (also called Alt-A mortgages) generally serve borrowers whose credit histories are close to prime, but the loans have one or more higher-risk characteristics such as limited documentation of income or assets or higher loan-to-value ratios;
- Subprime mortgages are generally made to borrowers with blemished credit and feature higher interest rates and fees than prime loans; and
- Government-insured or -guaranteed mortgages primarily serve borrowers who may have difficulty qualifying for prime loans and feature interest rates similar to those for prime loans. HUD's Federal Housing Administration (FHA), VA, and the Rural Housing Service operate major federal programs that insure or guarantee mortgages.

The nonprime market segment (Alt-A and subprime) features a number of nontraditional products and characteristics:

- Hybrid ARM—interest rate is fixed during an initial period, then "resets" to an adjustable rate for the remaining term of the loan.
- Payment-option ARM—borrower has multiple payment options each month, including negative amortization (minimum payments lower than needed to cover any of the principal or all the accrued interest, which may increase the outstanding loan balance over time).
- Interest-only—borrower can pay just the interest on the loan for a specified period, usually the first 3-10 years, thereby deferring principal payments.
- Low and no documentation loans—require little or no verification of a borrower's income or assets.

- High loan-to-value ratios—borrower would make a small down payment, causing the ratio of the loan amount to the home value to be relatively high. The higher the ratio when a loan is originated, the less equity borrowers will have in their homes.
- Prepayment penalties—borrower incurs a fee if he or she pays off the loan balance before it is due.
- Balloon payment loans—mortgages that do not fully amortize over the term of the loan, leaving a balance due at the end of the balloon period.

Mortgages can fall into any one of several payment status categories:

- Current—borrower has met scheduled payments.
- Delinquent—borrower has missed one or more scheduled monthly payments.
- Default—borrower is 90 or more days delinquent.[7]
- Foreclosure—borrower has been delinquent for more than 90 days and the lender has elected to initiate a legal process against the borrower that has several possible outcomes. Generally, the borrower loses the property because it is sold to repay the outstanding debt or is repossessed by the lender.
- Prepaid—borrower has paid the entire loan balance before it is due. Prepayment often occurs as a result of the borrower selling the home or refinancing.

After the loan has been made, originating lenders can retain their loans in portfolio or sell them to investors on the secondary market, either as whole loans to other financial institutions or (directly or indirectly through other financial institutions) as loan pools that are held in trusts and administered by a trustee.[8] The loan pools become asset-backed securities that are issued and sold to investors and are referred to as mortgage-backed securities. This process, often referred to as securitization (see figure 1), plays an important role in providing capital for mortgage lending by generating funds that can be used to originate more loans. Investors assume the interest rate, prepayment, and credit risk associated with the loans backing these securities, unless they are covered by mortgage insurance or guarantees on the securities.

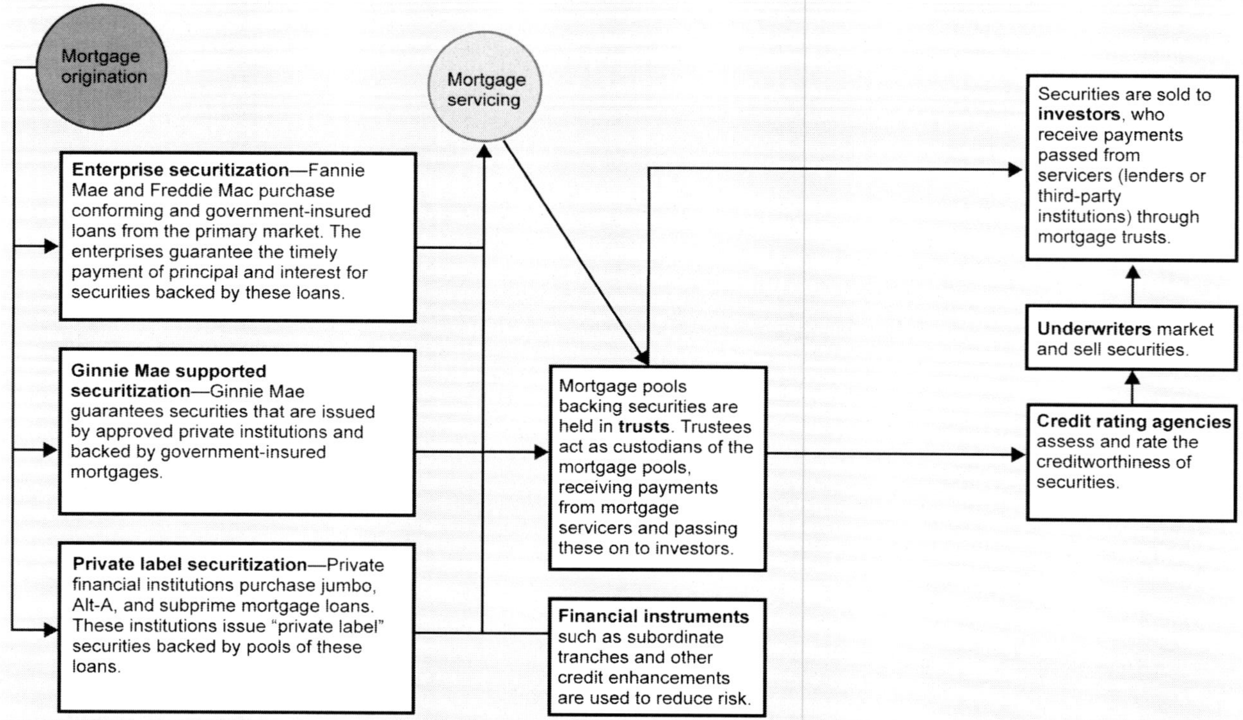


Source: GAO. | GAO-15-185

Figure 1. Mortgage Securitization Participants and Process.

The secondary market for residential mortgages consists of three major categories of securitizations—enterprise (Fannie Mae and Freddie Mac), Ginnie Mae, and private label. Fannie Mae and Freddie Mac are congressionally chartered, for-profit, shareholder-owned companies known as government-sponsored enterprises and have been under federal conservatorship since 2008.[9] They generally purchase conforming loans, which are mortgage loans that meet certain criteria for size, features, and underwriting standards.[10] In addition, the enterprises require that loans they purchase with loan-to-value ratios in excess of 80 percent have a credit enhancement mechanism, such as private mortgage insurance. Loans above this limit are known as jumbo loans. After purchasing mortgages, the enterprises create mortgage-backed securities and guarantee investors in these securities that they will receive timely payments of principal and interest. Ginnie Mae (a government corporation) guarantees securities that are issued by approved private institutions and backed by federally insured mortgages (FHA, VA, and USDA). Private institutions are also involved in the creation of private- label securities backed by mortgages that do not conform to the enterprises' purchase requirements (because the mortgages are too large or do not meet specified underwriting criteria). Private securitizing institutions include investment banks, retail banks, mortgage companies, and real estate investment trusts.[11]

Other participants to a private securitization transaction include, but are not limited to, credit rating agencies that assess the creditworthiness of the securities and deal with underwriters hired by securitizers to market and sell the securities to investors. Each type of securitization retains a mortgage servicer to collect mortgage payments from borrowers and disburse interest and principal payments to mortgage trustees, who pass them to investors. Servicers also manage delinquent loans that may lead to loss mitigation (such as a loan modification or a repayment plan) with the borrower or foreclosure.

## Ability-to-Repay and Qualified Mortgage Standards Rule

The ATR/QM regulations set forth minimum requirements lenders must consider in relation to making the required good faith determination of a consumer's reasonable ability to repay. To satisfy the ability-to-repay requirements, lenders generally must consider eight underwriting factors: (1) current or reasonably expected income or assets; (2) current employment status; (3) the monthly payment on the covered transaction (the monthly payment must be calculated based on any introductory rate or fully indexed rate for the loan, whichever is higher, and substantially equal, fully amortizing monthly payments); (4) the monthly payment on any simultaneous loan;[12] (5) the monthly payment for mortgage-related obligations; (6) current debt obligations, alimony, and child support; (7) the monthly debt-to-income ratio or residual income; and (8) credit history.[13] To satisfy the QM requirements, the loan must meet certain restrictions on product features and points and fees as well as meet certain underwriting requirements. The loan must not have risky features such as negative amortization, interest-only payments, or balloon payments (except in certain circumstances). The term of the loan should not exceed 30 years. Point and fees should be less than or equal to 3 percent of the loan amount (higher percentages are allowed for loans of less than $100,000). Finally, the loan also must meet certain underwriting requirements. The creditor must take into account the monthly mortgage payment utilizing a fully amortizing schedule using the maximum rate that may apply during the first 5 years after the first payment. The creditor must consider and verify income or assets and current debt obligations, alimony, and child support.

The rule also sets out three main categories of QMs that are presumed to comply with the ability-to-repay requirements: general, temporary, and small creditor.[14]

- Under the general category, all loans to borrowers with a monthly debt-to-income ratio of 43 percent or less that meet the restrictions on product features, points and fees, and underwriting requirements described above are QMs.
- Under the temporary category, loans that meet the restrictions on product features, and points and fees described above, and are eligible for purchase, insurance, or guarantee by Fannie Mae, Freddie Mac, FHA, USDA and its Rural Housing Service, or VA are QMs, but are not subject to a specific debt-to-income ratio.[15]
- Under the small-creditor category, loans must meet some restrictions on QMs such as product features and points and fees. Creditors must evaluate consumers' debt-to-income ratio or residual income, but the loans are not subject to a specific debt-to-income ratio. Generally, these loans must be held in portfolio by a small creditor for at least 3 years. However, there is another category for small creditors in rural and underserved areas in which mortgages with balloon payments originated by such creditors can be QM loans.[16]

If a lender originates a mortgage that meets the QM requirements and has an annual percentage rate (APR) within certain limits, the lender is presumed to have satisfied the ability-to-repay requirements and receives certain protections from liability. That is, these QMs have a safe harbor (a conclusive presumption that the lender has satisfied the ability-to-repay requirements) that immunizes the lender from claims related to the borrower's ability to repay.[17] Lenders still can receive some protection from liability if they originate higher-priced QMs (those with APRs above certain limits). That is, lenders are still presumed to have satisfied the ability-to-repay requirements, but borrowers can rebut the presumption. Borrowers can try to prove that based on information available to the lender at loan origination, the borrower would not have enough income left for living expenses after paying the mortgage and other debts.

Lenders also may make non-QM loans if they choose. However, these lenders will not benefit from the safe-harbor or rebuttable presumption liability protections afforded QM loans.

## Risk-Retention Rule and Qualified Residential Mortgages

The Dodd-Frank Act generally requires securitizers of asset-backed securities to retain not less than 5 percent of the credit risk of the assets collateralizing the security. The act includes exemptions, including one for securities collateralized exclusively by residential mortgages that are "qualified residential mortgages." The Dodd-Frank Act specifies that the QRM definition cannot be broader than the QM definition (that is, the QRM criteria can be more but not less restrictive than the QM criteria).

The act also requires agencies to specify

- criteria for QRMs, taking into consideration underwriting and product features that historical loan performance data indicate result in a lower risk of default;
- permissible forms of risk retention and the minimum duration for meeting the requirement;
- ways of allocating risk between securitizers and originators; and
- the possibility of permitting a lower risk-retention requirement (less than 5 percent) for any securitization collateralized by non-QRMs that meet underwriting standards the agencies develop in regulations.

In the final risk-retention rule, issued in December 2014, the QRM definition was aligned with the QM definition.[18] More specifically, loans that meet the QM requirements outlined previously are considered to be QRM loans. Thus, securities collateralized solely by QM loans (and therefore QRM loans) are not subject to risk-retention requirements. Congress intended the risk-retention regulations to help address problems in the securitization markets by requiring securitizers to retain an economic interest in the credit risk of certain assets they securitized. As a result, securitizers would have an incentive to monitor and ensure the quality of the assets underlying a securitization transaction, which also would help align their interests with the interests of investors.

In relation to risk retention, sponsors of securitizations will be required to retain at least 5 percent of the credit risk associated with a securitization that contains any non-QRM loans, unless an exemption applies. Under certain circumstances, sponsors may allocate the retention obligation to an originator, which agrees to retain that risk, if the originator has contributed at least 20 percent of the balance of a loan pool collateralizing mortgage-backed securities. The final rule requires this risk to be held by originators in the same way the risk was held by the securitizer.

## Role of Consumer Financial Protection Bureau

The Dodd-Frank Act transferred consumer protection oversight and other authorities over certain consumer financial protection laws from multiple federal regulators to CFPB. CFPB's responsibilities include

- ensuring that consumers are provided with timely and understandable information to make responsible decisions about financial transactions;
- ensuring that consumers are protected from unfair, deceptive, or abusive acts and practices, and from discrimination; and
- ensuring that markets for consumer financial products and services operate transparently and efficiently to facilitate access and innovation.

The Dodd-Frank Act also gave CFPB supervisory authority over certain nondepository institutions, including certain kinds of mortgage market participants. Such institutions generally lacked federal oversight before the financial crisis of 2007–2009.

Finally, the Dodd-Frank Act requires CFPB to conduct an assessment of each significant rule it adopts, such as the ATR/QM rule, and publish a report of the assessment no later than 5 years after the effective date of the rule.[19] For the ATR/QM rule, the due date is no later than January 10, 2019. The factors the assessments are to address include the rule's effectiveness in meeting the purposes and objectives of Title X of the Dodd-Frank Act.

### Retrospective Reviews of Regulations

Generally, Executive Orders and related implementation guidance from OMB require executive agencies and encourage independent regulatory agencies to develop and implement retrospective review plans.[20] In addition, OMB encourages agencies to preplan efforts to retrospectively review their regulations and give careful consideration about how best to promote empirical testing of the effects of rules both in advance and retrospectively.[21] OMB states that agencies may find it useful to engage in retrospective analyses of the costs and benefits (quantitative and qualitative) of regulations and suggests that independent regulatory agencies identify metrics to evaluate regulations and ensure they have high-quality data and robust models to conduct effective outcome-based reviews.[22] These directives and guidance also encourage agencies to solicit public comments and make the results of these reviews available to the public. Finally, agencies are encouraged to coordinate when conducting their retrospective reviews and consider the combined effects of their regulations.

## Mortgage Market Trends Generally Consistent with Tighter Underwriting Standards in Recent Years

During 2000-2014, originations for residential mortgage loans rose dramatically, then plummeted, and showed some signs of recovery in recent years. Available data indicate that low levels of riskier loan types have been originated since 2007. Additionally, measures of credit risk associated with mortgages, such as borrower credit scores and debt-to- income ratios, were consistent with an overall tightening of loan underwriting standards since 2008. The composition of the securities market for residential mortgages also changed during this period; in particular, the market share for private-label securities significantly diminished after 2007.

## Mortgage Market Indicators Suggest Some Recovery Has Begun

As shown in figure 2, mortgage origination volume peaked in 2003, sharply declined in 2008, and then remained above 2008 levels (with mixed increases and declines) through 2013 but declined in 2014—due to declines in refinancing. In dollar terms, origination volume declined from $3.7 trillion in 2003 to $1.2 trillion in 2014. The lower volume potentially indicates lower credit availability, decreased demand, or both. A range of factors contributed to mortgage market activity from 2000 through 2014.

### *Refinances*

During the years of rapidly increasing mortgage origination (2000–2003), decreasing interest rates and increasing home prices provided opportunities for borrowers to refinance to lower monthly payments or take equity out of their homes for consumption and investment.[23] As shown in figure 2, the volume of refinances increased to $2.8 trillion in 2003, and then decreased and remained at roughly $1.5 trillion from 2004 through 2007. Refinances as a percentage of mortgage originations peaked at 76 percent in 2003 and remained at roughly 70 percent from 2009 to 2013. Refinances declined to 44 percent in 2014. Similarly, the number of subprime cash-out refinances increased significantly from 2000 through 2005 (from about 246,000 in 2000 to about 1.2 million in 2005) and then declined to about 195,000 in 2007.

### *Mortgage Interest Rates*

Interest rates for mortgages trended downward for most of the period (2000–2014). As figure 2 illustrates, rates generally fell through 2004, increased gradually through 2007, generally declined through 2012, and then increased in 2013 and 2014. For example, the average 30-year fixed rate declined from 8.1 percent in 2000 to 3.7 percent in 2012 and rose to 4.2 percent in 2014. The pattern of mortgage rates roughly coincides with several actions the Federal Reserve took to lower the cost of credit during the recession.[24] For example, in November 2008 the Federal Reserve announced a program to purchase mortgage- backed securities backed by Fannie Mae, Freddie Mac, and Ginnie Mae, and had completed a total of $1.25 trillion in purchases in March 2010.[25] The goal of this program was to "reduce the cost and increase the availability of credit for the purchase of houses." The large-scale purchase program was an integral component of the Federal Reserve's efforts to ease financial conditions and provide policy accommodation in the crisis. Starting in September 2007 and on several occasions afterward, the Federal Reserve reduced the federal funds rate with the last reduction occurring in December 2008. Decreasing or increasing the federal funds rate—the rate at which depository institutions lend to other depository institutions overnight—can influence the cost and supply of credit, including mortgages.[26] Mortgage rates are generally a product of the supply of and demand for mortgages. Other factors, such as the prevalence of mortgage defaults, unemployment rates, and home prices also can determine the supply and demand for mortgages and thus also influence costs.

### *Default and Foreclosure*

Default and foreclosure rates peaked in 2010 but trended downward through 2013. From 2000 through 2006, mortgage performance was relatively stable. The rate of default was below 1 percent, and the foreclosure inventory rate—the percentage of total mortgage loans in foreclosure—was below 2 percent (see figure 2). These rates then rose to historic levels, the default rate reaching nearly 5 percent and the foreclosure inventory rate reaching 4.6 percent in the first quarter of 2010. Through 2013, the rates declined, suggesting some recovery in the housing and mortgage market. But at the end of 2013, the foreclosure inventory rate remained at 2.9 percent, according to data from the Mortgage Bankers Association. As we reported earlier, more aggressive lending practices—that is, an easing of underwriting standards and wider use of certain loan features associated with poorer loan performance—contributed to the increases in default and foreclosure rates that began in the third quarter of 2006.[27] In addition, the decline of house prices left borrowers more likely to have negative equity (owing more on a mortgage loan than the property is worth), which also contributed to the increases in defaults. Higher default rates may result in higher total losses for lenders on their loans.

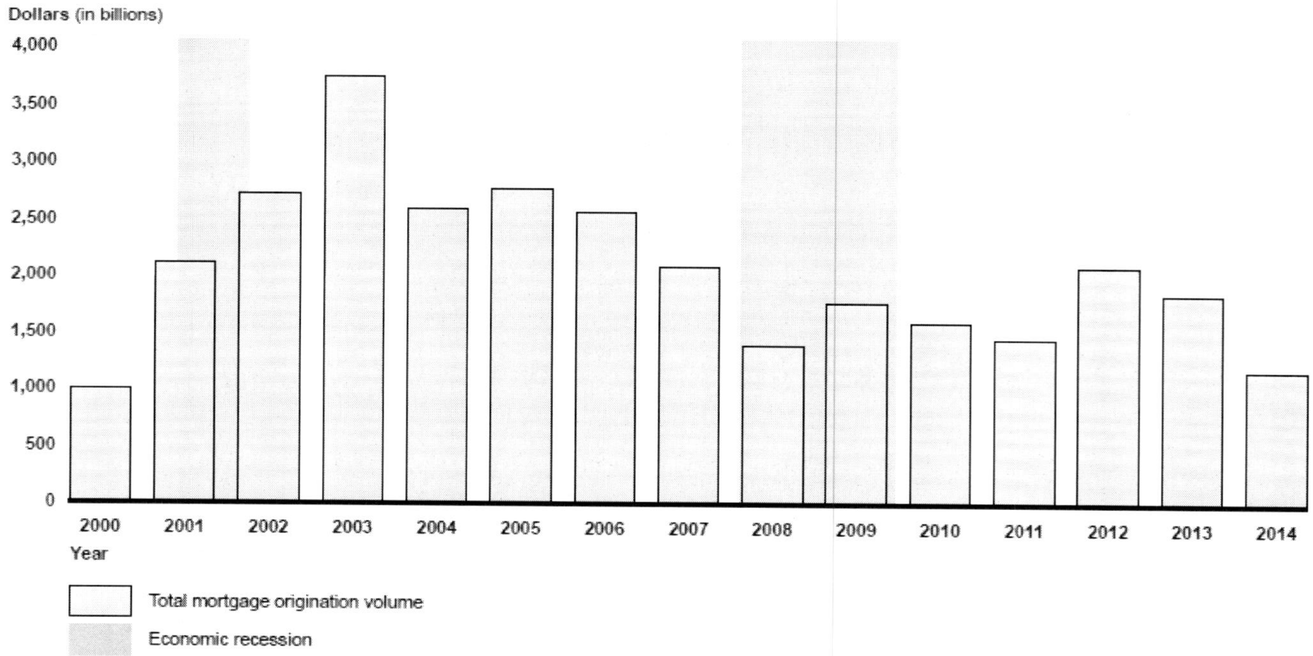


Source: GAO analysis of Inside Mortgage Finance and National Bureau of Economic Research data. | GAO-15-185

Figure 2. Mortgage Market Trends, Total Mortgage Origination Volume (2000-2014).

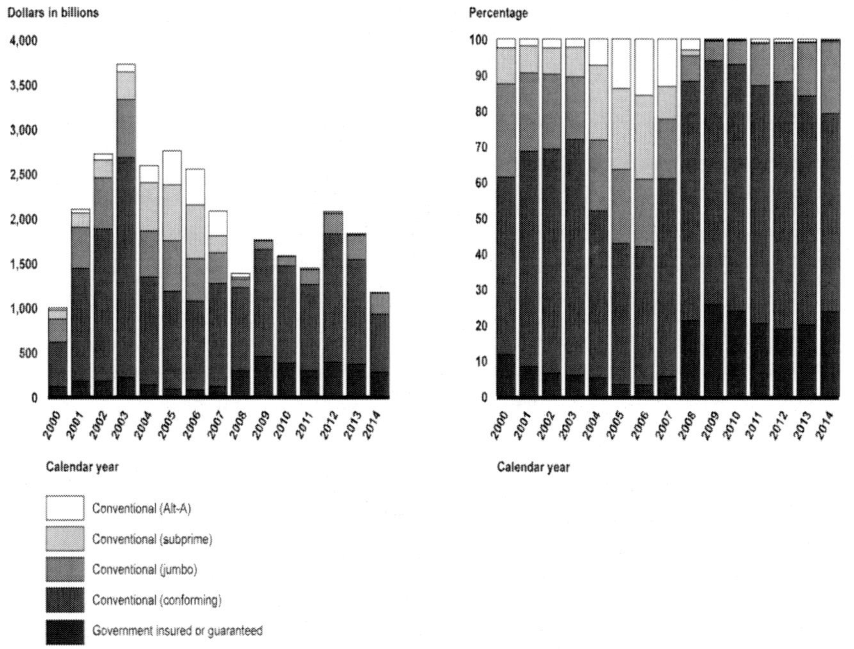


Source: GAO analysis of Inside Mortgage Finance data. | GAO-15-185

Notes: Conventional loans are mortgages that are not insured or guaranteed by the federal government. Other definitions for the data categories are the following: government-insured or guaranteed loans are loans insured or guaranteed by VA or FHA; conforming loans meet the requirements for purchase or securitization by Fannie Mae and Freddie Mac; jumbo loans are larger than the maximum eligible for purchase by Fannie Mae and Freddie Mac, not including Alt-A or subprime loans; Alt-A loans are made to prime-credit borrowers and have some combination of nontraditional documentation, nonstandard product structure, or more liberal underwriting; and subprime loans are made to those who have impaired credit.

Figure 3. Dollar Volume (in Billions) and Percentage of Single-Family Mortgage Originations, by Type (2000–2014).

## Low Levels of Riskier Loan Types Have Been Originated since 2007

Originations of riskier loan types declined to low levels after 2007. For example, the share of nonprime mortgages (Alt-A and subprime) decreased from about 40 percent in 2006 to less than 5 percent in 2008 (see figure 3). As noted in our 2009 report, the nonprime market segment featured a number of nontraditional products and characteristics.[28] Many of the features of these products, such as low or no documentation of borrower income and assets, are prohibited or limited under the final ATR/QM rule.

Since the decline in originations of riskier loan types, the market share of other loan types and products increased. For example, conforming and government-insured or guaranteed loans constituted the majority of loan originations from 2008 through 2014 (see figure 3). More specifically, such loans accounted for about 80 percent or more of the market during this period. Furthermore, the share of jumbo loans hit a low in 2009 (5.5 percent), and then generally increased through 2014 (20.1 percent).[29] Although larger than the conforming loan limit established by the enterprises, jumbo mortgages are generally considered prime mortgages and not Alt-A or subprime.

Although the data on ARMs with risky features are limited, those data suggest that the availability of these features declined between 2005 and 2007. For example, originations of subprime ARMs and Alt-A option ARMs increased rapidly from 2000 through 2005, but fell markedly in subsequent years. About 262,000 subprime ARMs were originated in 2000, but this number grew seven-fold to about 1.8 million originations in 2005 (the peak of the market for subprime ARMs).[30] By 2007, the number of these loans declined to about 214,000. Likewise, originations of Alt-A ARMs increased substantially, from about 10,000 loans in 2000 to more than 893,000 in 2005, but declined to about 249,000 by 2007. These nontraditional loans generally had fixed interest rates for short initial periods and then would convert to indexed rates higher than traditional ARMs—which could result in payment shock (large increases in monthly payments). Also, some lenders may have determined a borrower's ability to repay an ARM based on the initial monthly payment, rather than the higher payments if rates were to increase. As we and others have found, subprime hybrid and Alt-A option ARMs had significantly higher rates of serious delinquency (in default or foreclosure) than other subprime and Alt-A loans.[31]

## Since 2008, Measures of Credit Risk Associated with Mortgages Were Consistent with Tightening of Underwriting Standards

Since 2008, measures of the credit risk of purchase mortgages (such as borrower credit scores and debt-to-income ratios) were consistent with lenders tightening underwriting standards. Underwriting standards, such as those of FHA and the enterprises, include assessments of these measures. For example, the enterprises have a debt-to-income ceiling of 45 percent. A credit score is a numeric value that represents a borrower's potential credit risk, based on his or her credit history. Generally, a higher score indicates greater credit quality and potentially lower likelihood of default. Lenders continue to use credit scores as a primary means of assessing whether to originate a loan to a borrower.[32] As shown in figure 4, credit scores for purchase loans fluctuated but exhibited an upward trend since 2004. For example, average scores for these borrowers rose from 704 in January 2004 to 750 in December 2013.

As shown in figure 4, the average debt-to-income ratio for purchase loans increased to a high of about 40 percent in early 2008 and subsequently decreased to 34 percent in December 2013. Lenders use debt-to-income ratio as a key indicator of a borrower's capacity to repay a loan. The ratio represents the percentage of a borrower's income that goes toward all recurring debt payments, including the mortgage payment. A higher ratio is generally associated with a higher risk that the borrower will have cash flow problems and may miss mortgage payments.[33] A decline in debt-to- income ratios is consistent with a tightening of credit availability for borrowers with higher debt burdens. However, the data provider and others have noted that the data are often missing debt-to-income information and debt-to-income ratios are often calculated inconsistently. Nonetheless, research by CoreLogic suggests that lenders in recent years originated loans with lower debt-to-income ratios.[34]

Finally, average (mean) loan-to-value ratios for purchase loans increased since 2006. For example, from January 2003 to August 2006, average monthly loan-to-value ratios hovered around 80 percent. From September 2006 to November 2009, average monthly loan-to-value ratios increased about 5 percentage points to 85.6 percent. Since then, the ratios declined slightly, but remained higher than 2003–2006 levels. The continuing prevalence of higher ratios may be due in part to the increasing share of originations from FHA, which had an average loan-to-value ratio of about 96 percent for purchase loans originated from October 1999 to July 2014.[35] The lower ratios in 2003–2006 may have been due to the number of borrowers obtaining both first- and second-lien mortgages—"piggyback" loans—that may not be reflected in the previous statistics.[36] The higher the loan-to-value ratio when a loan is originated, the less equity borrowers will have in their homes and the more likely they are to default on mortgage obligations especially during times of financial stress.

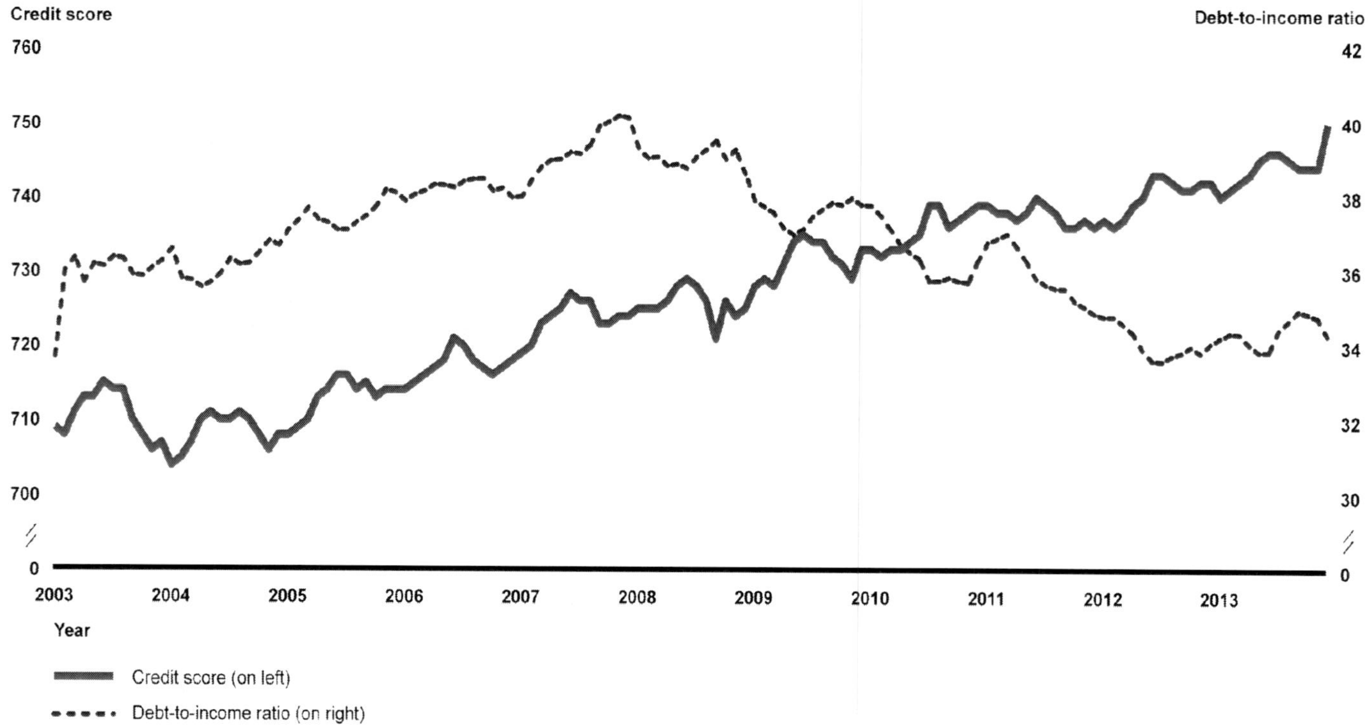


Source: GAO analysis of CoreLogic data. | GAO-15-185

Figure 4. Average Borrower Credit Score and Debt-to-Income Ratio for Single-Family Mortgage Originations (Purchase Loans Only), 2003–2013.

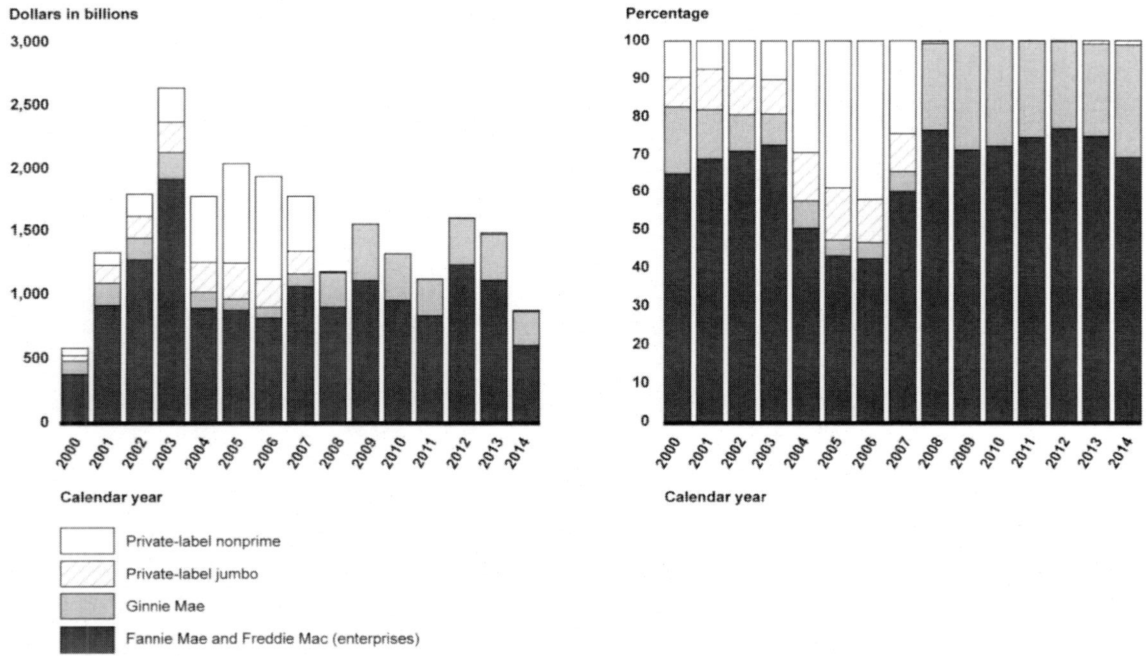


Source: GAO analysis of Inside Mortgage Finance data. | GAO-15-185

Figure 5. Value of Mortgage-Backed Securities Issued and Distribution of Market Share, in Billions, 2000–2014.

### Market Share for Private- Label Securities Significantly Diminished Since 2006

Securitization of residential mortgages changed significantly from 2000 through 2014. Mortgage-backed securities can be used by originators as a way of transferring risk (such as credit, prepayment, and interest rate risk) or to increase liquidity to help make additional loans. As shown in figure 5, the dollar volume of securitizations increased rapidly from 2000 to 2003, hit a low in 2008, and subsequently fluctuated. For example, $2.6 trillion of mortgages were securitized in 2003, compared to $874 billion in 2014. Market composition also changed dramatically during this period. Private-label securities, which typically pool jumbo and nonprime mortgages, represented more than half of mortgage securitizations in 2005 and 2006.[37] By 2008, private-label securitizations had declined to less than 1 percent of the market.

Decreased private-label issuances coincided with the decrease in Alt-A and subprime mortgages and a tightening of underwriting standards. As mortgage delinquencies and defaults rose for subprime and other mortgages, the losses were passed to investors. The increased losses likely contributed to the reduced demand for new issuances of private-label mortgage-backed securities. The growth in the market share of Ginnie Mae, Fannie Mae, and Freddie Mac resulted in part from actions by Congress and the Federal Reserve. Congress increased the loan limits for FHA-insured loans and loans eligible for securitization by the enterprises. As noted earlier, the federal government made explicit its backing of securities issued by the enterprises, and Ginnie Mae continued to provide federal guarantees for securities backed by government- insured mortgages. As noted earlier, the Federal Reserve provided additional support for the mortgage market by becoming one of the largest purchasers of securities issued by the enterprises and guaranteed by Ginnie Mae.[38]

## Initial Effects of Mortgage Regulations Likely Limited for Most Borrowers

Overall, agencies, market participants, and observers estimated that the QM and QRM regulations would not have a significant effect initially because many loans made in recent years already met QM and QRM criteria before these regulations were promulgated. Our review of economic analyses showed that researchers estimate that the majority of mortgages originated in recent years likely would have met the requirements for QM and QRM loans.[39] The recently finalized risk- retention rule aligns the definition of QRM with QM.

## Qualified Mortgage Regulations Likely to Have Limited Effects in Current Market

### *Availability of and Willingness to Originate Mortgages*

Estimates from the studies we examined pertaining to loans made in recent years suggest that if lenders continued current practices, a majority of loans would meet requirements for QM loans.[40] The studies used a variety of methodologies, including trend analysis with historical data, comparisons with established baselines, and surveys of market participants. Furthermore, in a July 2011 report, we found that the majority of loans originated from 2001 through 2010 would have met most of the individual QM criteria.[41]

Additionally, the different categories under which loans may qualify as QMs also suggest that the QM standards may have minimal effects on loan availability, at least in the short term. That is, not all loans that qualify as QM are subject to the same restrictions. For example, loans eligible for purchase by the enterprises or that have been federally insured or guaranteed are QMs under the temporary category and do not have to be at or under the 43 percent threshold for the debt-to-income ratio. As noted earlier, enterprise loans and those insured or guaranteed by the government (such as HUD and VA) held a dominant share of the market in recent years. Thus, some borrowers who may not qualify for QM loans subject to the 43 percent threshold may be able to acquire QM loans through these sources (current enterprise guidelines allow a debt-to- income ratio up to 45 percent). However, more of the market would be subject to the general threshold for a debt-to-income ratio of 43 percent once the temporary QM classification for loans eligible for sale to the enterprises ended. For example, the Federal Reserve estimated that 13 percent of Fannie Mae and Freddie Mac purchase mortgages had debt- to-income ratios above 43 percent in 2010.[42] In addition, there are adjustments to the QM definition for small creditors in rural and underserved areas. For example, balloon loans generally cannot be QMs; however, small-creditors operating predominantly in rural and underserved areas can make mortgages with balloon payments and those mortgages can qualify as QM loans.

Although the QM regulations were not expected to have a significant effect on the overall mortgage market initially, some researchers and participants estimated that they could adversely affect certain borrowers. For example, a study we reviewed indicated that a narrow debt-to-income threshold may disproportionately affect minorities and people living in high-cost areas.[43] Specifically, the higher cost of housing in certain areas can increase these ratios. In addition, some market participants raised the concern that lenders might be restricting lending to borrowers near the 43 percent debt-to-income or the 3 percent points and fees thresholds, out of concern that calculation errors could result in a non-QM loan.

The expectation of lower default rates for loans that meet the QM standards may make lenders more willing to originate QM than non-QM loans. Some researchers found that loans that appeared to meet the QM standards had a significantly lower default rate compared with loans that did not appear to meet the QM standards.[44] For example, one study found that 5.8 percent of loans made from 2000 through 2008 that appeared to meet the QM standards defaulted compared with an 11 percent rate for all loans made during that period. It also found higher default rates for Alt-A loans (22.3 percent) and subprime conventional loans (32.3 percent) during this period.[45] Another study found that while only 29 percent of loans originated between 2005 and 2008 did not appear to meet the QM standard, these loans represented 47 percent of all defaults during this period.[46] However, the study also found a number of performing loans that did not appear to meet the QM standard. Specifically, 25 percent of nondefaulting mortgages made between 2005 and 2008 did not appear to meet the QM standards.[47]

Some observers noted that because the QM standards do not include a measure of creditworthiness (such as credit score) or a loan-to-value ratio requirement, some QM loans may have characteristics associated with higher default rates. As we reported in 2005 and 2010, loans with higher credit scores, lower loan-to-value ratios, or both perform better than loans with low credit scores, higher loan-to-value ratios, or both, all else being equal.[48] Because non-QM loans present higher liability risks, lenders may impose stricter underwriting requirements for those loans, such as higher credit scores, lower loan-to-value ratio thresholds, or both.

Finally, studies that were conducted or posted after the implementation of the QM regulations anticipated or suggested moderate to minimal initial reductions in the availability of credit and willingness to originate non-QM loans. Two of these studies surveyed mortgage lenders and the other examined mortgage market trend data. Specifics of each study follow.

- A survey conducted in January and February of 2014 by the American Bankers Association when the QM regulations first took effect found that about 80 percent of respondents expected that the new regulations would have a measurable reduction in credit availability, and two-thirds of respondents characterized the impact as moderate.[49] The survey found mixed expectations on whether availability of all or only certain segments of mortgages would decline in response to the QM regulations. For example, 41 percent expected a reduction across all mortgages, and 40 percent of lenders expected a reduction only in non-QM lending. Furthermore, a third of lenders reported that they planned to restrict lending to QM segments only, and 29 percent indicated that they primarily would originate QM loans and only originate non-QM loans in targeted markets.[50]
- The Federal Reserve administered a survey of senior loan officers in July 2014 in which loan officers reported that approval rates decreased for some mortgage types in response to the ATR/QM regulations.[51] The survey found that the reductions in approval rates were often smaller for larger banks. Among the surveyed banks, the majority stated that approval rates did not decline for prime conforming loans, but about a third reported a reduction.[52] (Prime conforming loans include loans eligible for purchase by the enterprises—which include loans automatically designated as QM.) Among all banks surveyed that made nontraditional mortgages, more than half indicated that loan approval rates were lower for nontraditional purchase mortgages—which are often non-QM due to their product features—because of the ATR/QM regulations. Finally, more than half of the respondents indicated that the QM regulations had reduced application approval rates for prime jumbo home-purchase loans. However, in January 2015, another Federal Reserve survey of senior loan officers found that several large banks had eased lending standards for a number of categories of residential mortgages over the preceding 3 months, about 12 to 13 percent of the large banks surveyed indicated an easing of credit standards for QM and non-QM jumbo loans.[53]
- An article posted by the Urban Institute in August 2014 examined the effect the QM regulations might have on certain borrower and loan characteristics—such as borrowers with debt-to-income ratios above 43 percent, interest-only loans, adjustable-rate mortgages, and loans with small loan amounts—finding little variation in the proportion of

such loans before and after implementation of QM regulations.[54] For example, the share of loans with debt-to-income ratios above 43 percent remained relatively steady at approximately 17 percent for Fannie Mae and Freddie Mac loans, 35 percent for Ginnie Mae loans, and 10 percent for bank portfolio loans. However, from January through July 2014, the share of loans with higher debt-to-income ratios declined slightly for enterprise loans.

These statements and observations were made shortly after the QM regulation became effective.

### *Securitization of Mortgages*

Market participants with whom we spoke stated that the QM standards were unlikely to have a significant effect on the securitization of residential mortgages, largely because the majority of loans originated were expected to be QM loans. Representatives of credit rating agencies with whom we spoke indicated that they did not plan to require any additional credit enhancements when rating securities backed solely by QM safe-harbor loans.

Market observers, including two credit rating agencies also told us that there had been a relatively small volume (number and size) of private- label securitizations recently, consistent with the overall securitization trends we noted earlier. According to one of the larger credit rating agencies, the market issued 27 residential mortgage-backed securities in 2014, most of which contained only QM loans. Another larger credit rating agency told us that it rated 10 prime residential mortgage-backed securities in 2014 that included QM loans. Although three of the ten included non-QM loans, the proportion of non-QM loans was never greater than 2 percent in any transaction. Neither rating agency believed that a completely non-QM transaction was rated in 2014. Some observers told us that many non-QM loans originated after the QM regulations became effective had been held in portfolio, indicating they had not been securitized. However, observers noted that some securities have included non-QM loans and firms have discussed creating non-QM securities in the future.

### *Litigation and Compliance Costs of QM Regulations*

According to federal agency officials, the primary costs associated with the QM regulations are increased litigation and compliance costs. Generally, lenders, investors, and borrowers incur litigation costs when borrowers file a legal claim challenging a lender's efforts to assess the borrower's ability to repay. Lenders incur compliance costs to ensure that they comply with QM regulations, such as by documenting their efforts to assess borrowers' ability to repay.

Estimates for potential litigation costs associated with the QM regulations varied. Lenders' costs may increase due to potential litigation costs. The absence of safe harbor protection exposes higher-priced QM and non- QM loans to increased litigation risk.[55] Both CFPB and credit rating agencies estimated increased litigation costs associated with non-QM loans.[56] In contrast to CFPB, credit rating agencies also estimated increased litigation costs associated with higher-priced QM loans. However, CFPB stated that its estimated costs for nonqualified mortgages "should reasonably serve as an upper bound for the costs of qualified mortgages."[57] CFPB's estimate assumed that 20 percent of borrowers in foreclosure with non-QM loans would challenge a lenders' compliance with the ability-to-repay regulations. In contrast, the estimates of credit rating agencies about the probability of litigation ranged from 5 to 50 percent among borrowers in foreclosure with non-QM loans. Most significantly, the credit rating agencies considered if the borrower was located in a nonjudicial or judicial state.[58] CFPB also assumed that 20 percent of the borrowers challenging the lender would prevail in litigation. In contrast, the credit agencies' estimates for borrower success ranged from 10 to 75 percent.[59] Credit rating agencies estimates differed from CFPB's because of the different assumptions and methodologies used in their analyses.

Depending on the risk and costs to lenders associated with any additional litigation, they might manage these costs by passing them to borrowers in the form of higher loan costs or limiting the volume of loans originated that likely would be subject to litigation risk. For example, CFPB estimated that the potential for increased litigation costs would cause interest rates for non-QM loans to increase by approximately 2.5 basis points.[60] However, CFPB did not generate a similar estimate for high- priced QM loans. Following CFPB's rule, the credit rating agencies published credit enhancement adjustments, which are used to offset potential investor losses due to increased risk of litigation, for high-priced QM and non-QM loans. Fitch estimated an adjustment of 65 basis points for high-priced QM loans and 40 basis points for non-QM loans.[61] In contrast, Standard and Poor's estimated an adjustment of 9 basis points for high-priced QM loans and 30 basis points for non-QM loans.[62] Likewise, the addition of these credit enhancements ultimately may increase the cost of funding these loans.[63] The effect would be difficult to estimate because it is largely dependent on future housing market conditions, including the level of competition among lenders and among securitizers. Although these estimates provide insights about the costs associated with the QM regulations, agency officials and observers with whom we spoke said that the estimates were limited by the unique legal requirements for originators and investors under the Dodd-Frank Act that we discussed earlier. The observers noted that they expected to revise their estimates when litigation had taken place. Thus, the actual litigation costs associated with QM may not be known for some time.

Market participants and industry observers did not believe that compliance costs associated with the ATR/QM regulations would hinder the functioning of the overall market, but they identified compliance costs that were likely to be passed to consumers. For example, they noted that complying with the documentation standards creates additional work and adds processing time, both of which result in increased costs. Costs also could rise if institutions needed to take additional steps to properly disclose information in their financial statements about QM and non-QM loans. But market participants also noted that compliance costs may vary by institution and the degree to which an institution could realize certain economies of scale. Some indicated that compliance costs were significant for all originators, regardless of size, but added that these costs were related to more than just QM regulations, and included implementing Basel III standards.[64]

## Qualified Residential Mortgage Regulations Likely to Have Limited Effects in Current Secondary Market

### *Availability of Mortgages*

According to agency officials and observers, the QRM regulations, which were finalized in December 2014, were unlikely to have a significant effect on the availability of residential mortgages under current market conditions. A loan meeting QM standards automatically is QRM-eligible; therefore, securities collateralized solely by QM loans will not require securitizers to retain any of the risk. Securitizers generally must retain at least 5 percent of the credit risk associated with any securitization collateralized by any non-QRM loans. Securitizers may allocate the retention obligation to an originator, if the originator has contributed at least 20 percent of the balance of a loan pool collateralizing mortgage- backed securities. As discussed earlier, agency officials and market observers anticipate that the majority of loans will conform to QM standards and therefore believe that the QRM regulations will not have a substantial effect on the availability of residential mortgages for most borrowers.

### *Costs of Mortgages*

Since the risk-retention rule equated QRM with QM, mortgage market participants likely would incur few or low additional costs, if any, in ensuring that loans met the definition of QRM. As discussed earlier, the primary costs associated with the QM regulations are litigation and compliance costs. These additional costs may be passed to borrowers. To ensure compliance with the QRM regulations, lenders and securitizers might need to take additional steps to properly disclose information in their financial statements about QRM and non-QRM loans. According to the regulators, aligning the QRM definition with QM would meet the statutory goals and directives to limit credit risk and preserve access to affordable credit, while at the same time facilitating compliance. Specifically, the agencies in the final QRM regulations noted that the markets for those residential mortgages exempted under the final rule (that is, QRM mortgages) are expected to be large, and result in significant liquidity, economies of scale, and little-to-no impact on securitization of these mortgages. For non-QRM securities, the Federal Reserve estimated in October 2014 that a risk-retention requirement of 5 percent would add 25 basis points at most to a borrower's costs.[65] However, studies we reviewed and mortgage market participants with whom we spoke did not believe these costs would disrupt mortgage market function.

### *Securitization of Mortgages*

The effect of the QRM regulations on the securitization of residential mortgages is likely to be limited in the current market. By equating the definition of QRM with QM, the majority of loans currently being originated likely would be considered to be QRM-eligible and, therefore, not subject to risk retention. However, changes to the role of the federal government in relation to the structure of the market for residential mortgage-backed securities could change the expected effects of the QRM regulations. The final QRM regulations exempt certain securitizations from the risk- retention requirements, including securitizations that have the full guarantee of the enterprises and securitizations guaranteed by Ginnie Mae.[66] The enterprise exemption remains in effect only as long as Fannie Mae and Freddie Mac operate under federal conservatorship. This consideration is separate from the QM temporary exemption for enterprise loans discussed earlier.[67] According to Inside Mortgage Finance, the enterprises had a dominant share of the residential securitization market during 2013, with about 66 percent of mortgage originations made through the enterprises. Ginnie Mae guaranteed about 22 percent of the residential securitization market in 2013.

Market observers with whom we spoke did not anticipate that the QRM regulations would significantly limit the origination and securitization of most non-QRM loans in the current market. These observers, including the major banking associations, expected that the majority of non-QRM loans would be held in portfolio and not sold on the private-label secondary market, thus obviating the need for additional risk retention. Since the implementation of the QM regulations on January 10, 2014, the number and size of private-label securitizations have continued to be small compared with the volume and size of such securitizations from 2005 through 2007. According to the credit rating agencies with which we spoke, the majority of the loans that make up these recent securities met the QM definition and therefore would be considered to be QRM-eligible. Observers estimated that non-QRM loans sold to the private-label secondary market likely would be low-risk loans, such as interest-only loans to high-wealth borrowers.

However, some have cautioned that the equation of QM and QRM might restrict the secondary market for non-QRM loans and therefore limit the origination of these loans. For example, the risk-retention rule states that "the agencies recognize that aligning the QRM and QM definitions has the potential to intensify any existing bifurcation in the mortgage market that may occur between QM and non-QM loans, as securitizations collateralized by non-QMs could have higher funding costs due to risk- retention requirements in addition to potential risk of legal liability under the ability-to-repay rule."[68] The agencies acknowledged this risk but decided that not aligning QRM and QM definitions likely would result in even greater segmentation in the securitization market and higher costs for consumers. Furthermore, the final risk-retention rule requires that securitizations with blended pools of QRM and non-QRM loans be subject to the risk-retention requirements. As noted in the preamble to the rule, the QRM agencies (FDIC, Federal Reserve, FHFA, HUD, OCC, and SEC) anticipated that "QM and non-QM loans are less likely to be combined in a pool because of the different risk profiles and legal liabilities associated with these loans." Some industry observers pointed out that the small volume of non-QRM loans, which will be subject to risk-retention requirements, may not be sufficient to result in a fully functioning securitization market for such loans. Similarly, the preamble to the rule states that "securitization typically is a more cost-effective source of funding when the underlying pool includes a large number of loans." Although some private-label securities included both QM and non-QM loans in the same securitization in 2014, one rating agency noted that it had not rated any transactions that consisted entirely of non-QM loans and did not believe that such a transaction had closed during 2014. At least one sponsor plans to create a mortgage-backed security that is wholly non-QRM, according to one rating agency. Although some lenders have been making and holding non-QRM loans in their portfolios, the lack of a robust market for non-QRM securities may limit some lenders' willingness to underwrite non-QRM loans.

Some investors expressed the concern that the adopted QRM regulations did not increase investor protections for higher-risk loans that were QM-eligible. Specifically, the QRM regulations permit security sponsors to include QM-eligible loans with high-risk characteristics, such as high loan- to-value ratios and low credit scores, without imposing a risk-retention requirement. The risk-retention rule does not incorporate requirements for a loan-to-value ratio or a borrower's credit history because of concerns that the additional requirements might disproportionately affect low- and moderate-income, minority, or first-time homebuyers. Furthermore, the agencies believe the QRM requirements appropriately minimize regulatory compliance burdens in the origination of residential mortgage loans. According to an institutional investor advisor, investors would prefer to rely on risk retention as a method for holding mortgage originators and securitizers accountable. Outside of the risk- retention/QRM regulations, investors now have access to additional information that they could use to require sponsors to retain some of the credit risk of loans that make up the mortgage-backed security. Previously, investors typically lacked detailed information about the pool of loans that made up securities. However, SEC recently revised regulations for registered offerings of asset-backed securities to require that certain loan-level information for residential mortgage-backed securities (among other asset classes) be made available at the time of the offering and on an ongoing basis.[69]

## Efforts to Examine Effects of Both Regulations Faced Challenges

Due to the unavailability of certain important data elements, researchers faced challenges when analyzing the short-term and long-term potential effects of the QM and QRM regulations. Similarly, we previously reported that this issue makes evaluating the potential effects of the QM and QRM regulations difficult, as detailed in the following examples.[70]

- Debt-to-income ratios are key elements to identify QM and non-QM loans. However, as we and others have found, this information is often unreliable or missing.[71] Datasets frequently do not contain debt-to-income information for subprime and Alt-A loans, and available data often may be unreliable.[72]
- Information on the points and fees borrowers incur are also key elements to identify QM and non-QM loans. However, this information is not maintained in any available database, according to agency officials and observers. Without this information, it is difficult to determine if a loan complied with the QM requirement for a 3 percent cap on points and fees.

For these reasons, conclusively identifying the universe of QM loans is difficult. Instead, the studies must rely on other indicators of QM loans such as the lack of certain prohibited features or markers for the loan being fully documented.

Researchers also often faced challenges establishing a baseline for assessing the effect of the QM regulations. As discussed earlier, the housing market is highly cyclical, but the early 2000s saw a major expansion in many segments of the market. As such, the choice of a baseline can significantly affect a study's findings. For example, choosing an immediate precrisis baseline may make it appear that regulations were having a larger effect than they would with a postcrisis baseline. Baseline choices can result in different findings on the potential future effect of QM.

Mortgage market participants also told us that it would be difficult to isolate the effect of the regulations on the availability of mortgages because of other changes affecting the mortgage market. For example, many mortgage originators are also subject to the new CFPB servicing requirements.[73] As a result, it is difficult to attribute any changes observed in the mortgage market directly to the finalization of the QM and QRM regulations.

The long-term implications of the QM and QRM regulations on the mortgage market depend on several factors that are difficult to predict. For example, lender willingness to make non-QM loans (particularly to certain borrowers such as those with high debt-to-income ratios) and the cost of these loans are unknown. In addition, the future role of the enterprises in the residential mortgage market has yet to be determined and the mortgage activities of federal agencies may change (many proposals have been introduced to change the single-family housing finance system).[74] Moreover, the QM and QRM regulations may change over time. For example, CFPB took action to expand the exemption for small lenders after the rule had been finalized. Finally, the activities of nongovernmental and private participants can change over time

In a 2014 report that assessed protection for mortgage securities investors, we found that the ATR/QM regulations might set a floor to the loosening of credit and help prevent a repeat of the deterioration of lending standards that contributed to the 2007–2009 financial crisis.[75] The QM and QRM regulations provide incentives to originate QM and QRM loans. For example, originating a QM loan provides litigation protection for the lender and assignee if the loan is sold to an investor. Similarly, securitization sponsors are not required to retain any portion of the credit risk of QRM loans if the securitization exclusively comprises QRM loans. Should underwriting standards begin to loosen and lenders become more willing to offer loans that do not meet QM or QRM standards, these incentives may deter some lenders from loosening standards beyond the limits specified in the regulations. Although the regulations may help limit high-risk mortgage lending in future market expansions, some activities are not forbidden by statute (for example non-QM mortgage loans still can have negative amortization and interest-only payments). Nonetheless, lenders must assess the borrowers' ability to repay for all loans, including any non-QM loans lenders may originate and sponsors may securitize.

## PLANNING FOR REVIEWS OF REGULATIONS LACKED KEY ELEMENTS

CFPB and HUD have begun planning for their reviews of the QM regulations. CFPB identified potential outcomes, data sources, and analytical methods for examining its QM regulations, but had not finalized its plans. HUD identified outcomes and potential data sources, but had not identified specific metrics, baselines, and analytical methods for examining its regulations.[76] The agencies responsible for the QRM regulations identified outcomes and potential data sources and analytical methods, but had not yet identified specific metrics and baselines for examining the QRM regulations.

## CFPB Had Not Completed Plan That Specified Outcomes and Methodologies

In response to the Dodd-Frank requirement to review significant rulemakings, CFPB has made efforts to identify data, but as of May 2015 had not finalized a plan that specified what outcomes and methodologies—such as metrics, baselines, and analytical methods—it will use to examine the effects of the QM regulations. CFPB discussed some potential plans to review the QM regulations in the final ATR/QM rule but has not since finalized a plan for its analysis.

The Dodd-Frank Act requires CFPB to assess "the effectiveness of the rule or order in meeting the purposes and objectives of this title [Title X— Bureau of Consumer Financial Protection] and the specific goals stated by the Bureau." Furthermore, Executive Order 13563 states that the regulatory system "must measure, and seek to improve, the actual results [outcomes] of regulatory requirements."[77] But CFPB has not yet completed plans for how it intends to examine the QM regulations. For instance, a review addressing the purposes of the title might include outcomes such as the effects of the regulations on the overall housing market, cost or availability of credit to borrowers, regulatory burden on industry participants, or protection of consumers from unsustainable mortgage products. The choice of outcomes to be examined plays a key role in the selection of appropriate or relevant data, baselines, and analytical methods. For example, examining the cost and availability of mortgage credit could require different data elements and analysis than examining the effectiveness of the QM regulations in preventing defaults and foreclosures.

To date, CFPB has identified several potential data sources it could use to examine the QM regulations. For example, CFPB identified data collected to meet the requirements of the Home Mortgage Disclosure Act (HMDA).[78] HMDA data currently include information about mortgage applications, originations, and loans purchased on the secondary market. However, HMDA currently does not contain information to determine if a loan is QM or non-QM. The Dodd-Frank Act directs CFPB to expand HMDA data reporting requirements. For example, it directs the collection of points and fees information, interest rate spreads, and certain other loan features.[79] CFPB also has proposed to collect additional information (such as borrowers' debt-to-income ratios and whether the loan meets the QM standard) that could be used to examine the QM regulations. However, the data elements may not be finalized as proposed and may not be available at the time CFPB conducts its analysis (the report on the review must be published no later than Jan. 10, 2019). CFPB had not finalized the HMDA proposal as of April 2015.[80] Once the new HMDA reporting requirements are finalized, CFPB officials said lenders will need time to modify their systems to comply with the new reporting requirements, collect the data, and report the data to CFPB.[81] CFPB officials indicated that the earliest the new data might be collected would be in 2017. Moreover, HMDA data do not include and are not planned to include information about the performance of loans—such as default, delinquency, and foreclosure.[82] According to agency officials, loan performance information would be important to fully examine the effects of the QM regulations.

CFPB also entered into a partnership with FHFA to build the National Mortgage Database (NMDB), which will contain loan-level information about the mortgage, borrower, and property for a nationwide sample of 5 percent of borrowers from credit bureau files.[83] FHFA officials said information from a credit bureau (such as borrowers' credit scores and payment history on the mortgage) will be supplemented with data from other sources, such as HMDA and property valuation models, to create a comprehensive profile for each mortgage in the database. FHFA officials said NMDB is planned to include borrower's debt-to-income ratios, points and fees, interest rate of the loan, and information on loan performance. Although the data used to create NMDB includes personally identifiable information, the database will not contain personally identifiable information, according to CFPB officials. The database is not yet available. FHFA officials anticipated merging the data sources in 2015 and conducting analyses using the database at the end of 2015 or 2016. FHFA officials have noted some concerns about the reliability of some of the data, such as inconsistent definitions used for the debt-to-income ratio at loan origination. Furthermore, many loan records do not contain any information for some data elements, such as debt-to-income ratio. Ultimately, FHFA officials hope to obtain debt-to-income information from HMDA, which they anticipate will be a reliable data source. But, as noted earlier, the expanded HMDA data will not be collected until at least 2017.

CFPB also discussed using data to which it already has access, such as datasets from CoreLogic and BlackBox LLC.[84] These two data sources contain data similar to HMDA (such as origination data) and the forthcoming NMDB (such as loan performance information). CFPB suggested that it could use these datasets to conduct analysis similar to the one it conducted when developing the ATR/QM rule. For example, CFPB used data from the two private vendors to estimate the percentage of loans that would have qualified as QMs from 1997 through 2003 and in 2011. However, according to CFPB officials, CoreLogic and BlackBox LLC data do not contain any information on points and fees or reliably contain borrowers' debt-to-income ratios. CFPB officials said they could estimate the points and fees by deriving them from the stated interest rate and APR of the loan, but cautioned that determining what charges were included in the APR calculation was complex. Any analyses utilizing this approach would need to consider and potentially correct for any bias in the missing data.

CFPB officials said they have been collecting qualitative information from various sources to monitor the initial effects of the QM regulations on the residential mortgage market. For example, CFPB officials said they have been tracking industry news, reviewing reports from media outlets, and reviewing reports published by institutions and market participants (such as credit rating agencies and some lenders) and the Federal Reserve. In addition, CFPB officials said they have held informal conversations with lenders at industry events and conferences to obtain their views on the effects of the QM regulations. CFPB officials said this information alone would not be enough to examine the QM regulations, but would inform their approach for examining the regulations.

OMB encourages agencies to preplan efforts to retrospectively review their regulations to improve the effectiveness of the reviews.[85] OMB suggests that agencies identify metrics to evaluate regulations, identify baselines for their planned analyses, and ensure they have robust models to conduct their analyses.[86] Furthermore, when promulgating regulations, OMB encourages agencies to give careful consideration about how to promote empirical testing of the effects of the rules during retrospective reviews.[87] We found in a July 2007 report that agencies would be better prepared to undertake reviews if they identified what data and measures would be needed to assess the effectiveness of a rule before they started a review and, indeed, before they promulgated the rule.[88]

CFPB officials told us that they had not yet finalized a plan for their retrospective review because they had been focusing first on developing and finalizing the mandated regulations. Congress required CFPB to issue the QM regulations within 18 months of the "designated date" for the transfer of consumer financial protection functions under section 1061 of the Dodd-Frank Act to CFPB from other agencies.[89] CFPB officials told us that a plan to assess the QM regulations is critical. But, as of May 2015, CFPB officials were working to finalize a review plan and officials could not tell us what outcomes they would measure and what data and methodologies they would use to examine the effectiveness of these regulations. Without a plan to assess the

QM regulations, CFPB may be limited in its ability to effectively examine the regulations by the mandated deadline. Such a plan will be particularly important because of the uncertainty about the availability and timing of needed data, which may necessitate consideration of alternative analytic strategies and data sources.

## HUD Had Not Specified Methodologies to Conduct Analysis

HUD identified how it intends to examine its QM regulations and some potential data sources, but the agency has not yet determined how it would measure the effects of these regulations, including metrics, baselines, and analytical methods. Although the Dodd-Frank Act does not require HUD to conduct an assessment of its QM rule, HUD in its final rule stated that it would further study the parameters for distinguishing between safe harbor and rebuttable presumption QM for loans subject to its QM regulations. However, the final rule did not specify a time frame for that study. HUD also noted in the final rule that it would add the issue of whether to use a residual income test in its QM regulations to its agency-wide plan for retrospective review of regulatory actions.[90] Lenders can use a borrower's residual income as one measure of ability to make a mortgage payment.[91]

HUD does not maintain key data that it would need to conduct the reviews—such as information on points and fees and interest rate spreads (criteria for determining if a loan is safe harbor or rebuttable presumption) and data needed to calculate residual income. To mitigate the data gaps, HUD officials said they have considered using HMDA and NMDB data. But as we discussed previously, the availability dates of the expanded HMDA and NMDB data—such as information on points and fees—are not known. As of May 2015, the agency also had not identified how it would measure the effects of these regulations, including metrics, baselines, and analytical methods.

HUD officials stated that they have not finalized plans for their review of the QM regulations because of the uncertainty about the availability of data resources, such as NMDB. They noted that once the NMDB database was released, they would be able to determine whether it could be used as a resource to monitor and examine QM lending. But, without a plan to identify how to obtain necessary data and identify metrics, baselines and analytical methods, HUD may be limited in its ability to effectively review its regulations and achieve the intended outcomes of its reviews.

## Agencies Have Not Yet Specified Methodologies and Collaborative Strategies for QRM Reviews

Agency efforts to assess the QRM regulations included identifying outcomes and potential data sources and methodologies, but have not yet identified specific metrics, baselines, or analytical methods. The six agencies responsible for the QRM regulations—FDIC, FHFA, Federal Reserve, HUD, OCC, and SEC—have committed to commence a review of the QRM definition no later than 4 years after the effective date of the final rule (Dec. 24, 2015, for the QRM-related provisions), and every 5 years thereafter. In the risk-retention final rule, the agencies recognized that mortgage and securitization market conditions and practices change over time, and therefore stated it would be beneficial to review the QRM definition. More specifically, the agencies would consider the structures of securitizations, roles of the various transaction parties, relationships between enterprise and private-label markets, and trends in mortgage products in various markets and structures. They also stated that they would review how the QRM definition affected residential mortgage underwriting and securitization under evolving market conditions.[92] The agencies noted the timing would help ensure the initial review of the QRM definition benefitted from CFPB's review of the ability-to-repay rules, including the QM definition, and would help the agencies in determining whether the QRM definition should continue to fully align with the QM definition in all aspects.

Agency officials said their efforts have included identifying potential data sources for the review of the QRM regulations. For example, they noted that they likely would use mortgage data sources similar to those utilized when developing the QRM regulations, such as loan-level data from the enterprises and information on private-label mortgage-backed securities from a private data vendor. However, agency officials acknowledged that the data available from these sources are missing key information, such as points and fees and borrower's debt-to-income ratios, needed to determine if a loan is QM or non-QM, and consequently QRM eligible. In addition, agency officials identified HMDA and NMDB as possible data sources. However, the databases currently do not collect information on points and fees and debt-to-income ratios, which may limit their usefulness for examining the QRM regulations. Finally, the agencies have considered using data collected through the Fannie Mae Mortgage Lender Sentiment Survey and the Mortgage Bankers Association's Mortgage Credit Availability Index to help examine the QRM definition.[93] Although agency officials have identified several data sources, they have not established which data elements to select or how they would be used to assess the QRM regulations.

Agency officials said their efforts also have included identifying potential methodologies to assess the QRM regulations. For example, they plan to use information collected through their ongoing efforts to monitor broad trends and developments in the residential mortgage market, such as mortgage applications, originations, products, and securitizations as well as loan performance. They also have considered examining loan volumes for QRM and non-QRM loans, as well as QM safe harbor and rebuttable presumption loans. Furthermore, they may conduct a trend analysis by comparing market data before and after the risk-retention rules were effective. Finally, they said that they may look at early payment delinquencies and defaults of newly originated mortgages, as well as different kinds of QM loans, such as those covered under the QM temporary exemption for enterprise loans.

Although the agencies identified several retrospective review components—such as outcomes to examine and potential data sources and methodologies—they have not developed a plan that identifies specific metrics and baselines or committed to specific analytical methods. Agency officials stated that they have not developed more specific plans because their ongoing efforts to monitor broad mortgage market trends were sufficient. Additionally, agency officials expected additional information on the housing and mortgage market to be available for their review of the QRM regulations. They explained that the information would be important in determining whether the QRM definition was appropriate under prevailing market conditions. However, the timing, accuracy, and completeness of the data that may be available in time for the agencies to conduct their retrospective reviews (commencing no later than Dec. 24, 2019) are unclear. As we discussed previously, agencies can be better prepared to undertake their reviews and may be able to overcome or mitigate data challenges by identifying specific data sources, metrics, baselines, and analytical methods well before conducting the review, ideally before promulgating the rule.

Moreover, although agency officials acknowledged that the review of the QRM regulations necessitates interagency collaboration and plan to collaborate, the agencies have not yet identified specific mechanisms to promote effective collaboration. According to agency officials, the QRM agencies and CFPB held interagency meetings as agreed to during the promulgation of the QM and QRM regulations. The agencies plan to hold interagency meetings to conduct the reviews of the QRM regulations.

OMB guidance encourages agencies with overlapping jurisdiction or expertise to determine how the agencies will coordinate to conduct retrospective reviews.[94] In prior reports, we identified key practices to effective agency collaboration, including (1) agreeing on agency roles and responsibilities, (2) defining and articulating a common outcome, (3) establishing mutually reinforcing or joint strategies, and (3) identifying and addressing needs by leveraging resources.[95] Without establishing a framework for collaboration, such as specifying the roles each will play and responsibilities, the agencies involved in the QRM reviews may be limited in their ability to measure the effects of the regulations within the established time frames for their review.

## CONCLUSIONS

In promulgating the QM and QRM regulations, the federal agencies attempted to balance the goals of protecting borrowers and investors from the abuses that contributed to the recent housing crisis with the goal of maintaining access to affordable credit. While the QM and QRM regulations likely will have limited initial effects in the current mortgage market, the long-term implications of the regulations on the mortgage market depend on several factors that are difficult to predict. As such, it will be important for the agencies to conduct retrospective reviews of these regulations. However, federal agencies' efforts to prepare for examining the QM and QRM regulations have not yet incorporated some important elements of effective reviews as described below.

- Although CFPB, HUD, and the QRM agencies identified potential data sources (such as HMDA and NMDB), these data sources do not maintain information needed to reliably identify QM and QRM loans. CFPB and FHFA have been taking steps to expand these data sources. However, it is not clear if the expanded data will be available for the initial reviews.
- HUD has not identified specific metrics, baselines, or analytical methods to conduct its analyses
- Although the QRM agencies identified potential analytical methods to conduct their analyses, they have not identified specific metrics and baselines.

- The six agencies conducting the review of the QRM regulations have not specified mechanisms to promote effective collaboration, such as agreements on agency roles and responsibilities.

Finalizing plans to retrospectively review the mortgage regulations and incorporating these key elements will better position the agencies to measure the effects of the regulations and identify any unintended consequences. The agencies also could better understand data limitations and methodological challenges and have sufficient time to develop methods to deal with these limitations and challenges. Furthermore, the QRM agencies could identify opportunities to effectively collaborate and assign duties and responsibilities to help ensure effective use of available resources.

## RECOMMENDATIONS FOR EXECUTIVE ACTION

We are making the following three recommendations.

To enhance the effectiveness of its preparations for conducting a retrospective review of its QM regulations, CFPB should complete its plan. The plan should identify what outcomes CFPB will examine to measure the effects of the regulations and the specific metrics, baselines, and analytical methods to be used. Furthermore, to account for and help mitigate the limitations of existing data and the uncertain availability of enhanced datasets, CFPB should include in its plan alternate metrics, baselines, and analytical methods that could be used if data were to remain unavailable.

To enhance the effectiveness of its preparations for conducting a retrospective review of its QM regulations, HUD should develop a plan that identifies the metrics, baselines, and analytical methods to be used. Furthermore, to account for and help mitigate the limitations of existing data and the uncertain availability of enhanced datasets, HUD should include in its plan alternate metrics, baselines, and analytical methods that could be used data were to remain unavailable.

To enhance the effectiveness of their preparations for conducting a retrospective review of the QRM regulations, the agencies responsible for the QRM regulations—FDIC, FHFA, Federal Reserve, HUD, OCC, and SEC—should develop a plan that identifies the metrics, baselines, and analytical methods to be used and specify the roles and responsibilities of each agency in the review process. Furthermore, to account for and help mitigate limitations of existing data and the uncertain availability of enhanced datasets, the six agencies should include in their plan alternate metrics, baselines, and analytical methods that could be used if data were to remain unavailable.

## Agency Comments and Our Evaluation

We requested comments on a draft of this report from CFPB, FDIC, Federal Reserve, FHFA, HUD, OCC, and SEC. We received written comment letters from each of the seven agencies. We also received technical comments from the agencies (except OCC) that we incorporated as appropriate.

In response to our QM-related recommendations, CFPB concurred and HUD agreed with the draft report recommendations in their comment letters. CFPB stated that it was on track to finish its retrospective review on time. In addition, CFPB provided additional details about the general approach, data, metrics, and analytical methods that were likely to be used in its review. To better recognize these planning steps, we expanded our description of CFPB's planning efforts, and modified the recommendation to emphasize that CFPB should complete its plan.

In response to our QRM-related recommendations, two of the six agencies (HUD and FDIC) stated that they agreed with the recommendations in their comment letters. The other four agencies (the Federal Reserve, FHFA, OCC, and SEC) did not explicitly agree with our recommendations but outlined activities or efforts related to planning for the retrospective review of the QRM definition. For example, the agencies discussed their ongoing data analysis of mortgage market trends and efforts to identify sources for data not currently available, such as debt-to- income ratios and points and fees. Furthermore, SEC identified several potential metrics it could use to examine the QRM definition. For example, SEC expects to examine delinquencies by debt-to-income ratios, among other things. The Federal Reserve noted that it was fulfilling much of our recommendation as part of its regular business operations. However, the agencies did not provide specific time frames for finalizing their approach for the retrospective reviews or how they plan to address uncertainty about the availability of key data needed for the review, such as debt-to-income ratios. For example, the Federal Reserve and SEC stated that their precise analytical approach to reviewing the definition of QRM will depend on data availability and mortgage market conditions. Additionally, all the agencies indicated that they planned to work collaboratively in conducting their retrospective reviews. FHFA and OCC stated they planned to begin preparing for the review after the QRM definition was effective (December 2015). Finally, two letters identified some mechanisms that could promote effective collaboration. For example, FDIC and SEC noted that the agencies intended to divide responsibilities according to agency expertise and resources.

But the agencies could and should be doing more to finalize their plans to retrospectively review the mortgage regulations. As we discussed in the draft report, agencies can be better prepared to undertake their reviews and may be able to overcome or mitigate data challenges by identifying specific data sources, metrics, baselines, and analytical methods well before conducting the review, ideally before promulgating the rule. It will be particularly important to have plans that address these elements because of the uncertainty about when and if needed data will be available, which may necessitate consideration of alternative analytic strategies and data sources Incorporating these key elements also will better position the agencies to measure the effects of the regulations and identify any unintended consequences.

The comment letters of the agencies involved in the QRM reviews also outlined a general approach to collaboration. However, without establishing a specific framework for collaboration, such as specifying the roles each agency will play and their responsibilities and defining and articulating a common outcome, the agencies involved in the QRM reviews may be limited in their ability to measure the effects of the regulations within the established time frames for their review.

Mathew J. Scirè
Director, Financial Markets and Community Investment

## APPENDIX I: OBJECTIVES, SCOPE, AND METHODOLOGY

This report (1) describes selected trends in the origination and securitization of residential mortgages in 2000–2014; (2) discusses the expected effects of the qualified mortgage (QM) and qualified residential mortgage (QRM) regulations on the residential mortgage market; and (3) examines the extent to which federal agencies have plans in place to monitor and assess the effects of the QM and QRM regulations on the residential mortgage market.

## Trends in the Origination and Securitization of Residential Mortgages

To describe trends of residential mortgages from 2000 through 2014, we reviewed a range of mortgage market data generated by federal agencies, mortgage market participants, and observers and identified indicators that may be useful to gauge the effects of QM and QRM regulations. We selected indicators associated with the origination and securitization of residential mortgages (including the volume of originations by certain characteristics, interest rates, foreclosure and default rates, and volume of mortgage-backed security issuances) that are described below:

- To describe the volume of mortgage originations by certain characteristics, we relied on summary data published by Inside Mortgage Finance and data provided by CoreLogic LLC.[96] For example, we examined Inside Mortgage Finance data describing the volume of originations by loan type—including conventional conforming, Alt-A, subprime, jumbo, and government-insured; type of interest rate (fixed- and adjustable-rate); and loan purpose (purchase and refinance).[97] The Inside Mortgage Finance summary data do not include loans guaranteed by the Department of Agriculture. We did not independently confirm the accuracy of the Inside Mortgage Finance data. To determine the reliability of the data, we reviewed publicly available information on the data source and queried a knowledgeable official about the accuracy of the data. In addition, we examined CoreLogic LLC data describing the volume of loan originations by borrowers' credit score, debt-to-income ratio, and loan- to-value ratio. The CoreLogic summary data include conventional loans as well as loans insured or guaranteed by the Federal Housing Administration and other federal programs. These data are restricted to first-lien mortgages for the purchase of properties. CoreLogic officials estimated 99 percent of the loans were for single-family residential properties (1-4 units). These data provide wide coverage of the national mortgage market—that is, approximately 85 percent of mortgages, according to CoreLogic officials. Due to the proprietary nature of CoreLogic's estimates of its market coverage, we could not directly assess the reliability of this estimate. We have used CoreLogic data in prior reports in which we concluded the data were sufficiently reliable for our purposes.[98]

Nevertheless, because of limitations in the coverage and completeness of the data, our analysis may not be representative of the mortgage market as a whole. To determine the reliability of the CoreLogic data, we reviewed information on the data source and queried a knowledgeable official about the process CoreLogic used to collect its data and generate the summary data. Although the CoreLogic data have certain limitations—for example, certain data fields are not fully reported—we concluded that the data we used were sufficiently reliable for our purposes.

- To describe mortgage interest rates, we relied on published data in Freddie Mac's Primary Mortgage Market Survey. To determine the reliability of these data, we reviewed publicly available information on the data source. We determined the data were sufficiently reliable for our purpose, which was to provide information about how residential mortgage interest rates had changed over the relevant time period.
- To describe the volume of mortgages in default and foreclosure and recession periods, we relied primarily on a prior GAO report that identified and analyzed key national housing market indicators.[99] We used data collected for the prior report and reviewed our prior data reliability assessment. Based on this review, we determined that the data were reliable for our purposes. To update the data and analyses, we relied on several data sources including the National Delinquency Survey data issued by the Mortgage Bankers Association, and data issued by the National Bureau of Economic Research. Generally, we updated our assessments of the reliability of these data by reviewing existing information about data quality and corroborating key information. We determined that the data were sufficiently reliable for our purposes.
- To describe the volume of mortgage-backed security issuances, we relied on summary data published by Inside Mortgage Finance. We did not independently confirm the accuracy of the data we obtained. However, we reviewed publicly available information on the data source and queried a knowledgeable official about the accuracy of the data. We determined these data were sufficiently reliable for our purposes.

## Expected Effects of the QM and QRM Regulations

To discuss the expected effects of the QM and QRM regulations on the residential mortgage market, we identified and reviewed 24 economic analyses examining the potential effects of these regulations. We identified these analyses through means that included consultation with subject-matter experts (internal and external to GAO), electronic searches of scholarly databases, and reviews of studies conducted by agencies to inform the rulemakings. Generally, the analyses examined the effects the regulations may have on the cost, origination, availability, and securitization of residential mortgages and were performed by federal agencies, academics, industry observers, and industry participants. To review the 24 analyses, we designed a data collection instrument to ensure we collected consistent information from each. To develop the data collection instrument we identified important characteristics for high-quality analyses from sources that included internal GAO guidance on reviewing economic analyses and other federal requirements and best practices for conducting economic reviews during the rulemaking process. GAO staff separately subjected each analysis to a primary and secondary review and independently verified that the collected information was accurate. The staff also used the data collection instrument to identify methodologies and any methodological concerns that may have precluded us from using the economic analyses. We did not exclude any of the economic analyses from our review. The team reviewed the information collected to identify trends across the analyses and identify estimated effects of the regulations. We believe the economic analyses are generally reliable for reporting the range of estimates of the effects of the regulations. We noted instances in which the analyses may have had methodological challenges or data were either missing or unreliable. We discussed any specific concerns about methodology or scope in this report. In addition to the 24 analyses, we reviewed three studies on the initial effects of the QM regulations that were conducted after the rule became effective.[100] (See app. II for a list of the 27 studies we reviewed.) We did not apply our data collection instrument to these studies, but reviewed the findings and the methodologies of these studies. We believe the three studies were sufficiently reliable for the purposes of describing immediate effects of the QM regulations.

We also reviewed additional sources that contained information about potential effects of the QM and QRM regulations on the residential mortgage market. For example, we reviewed *Federal Register* releases and comment letters associated with the promulgation of the QM and QRM regulations. We also interviewed agency officials, stakeholders, and others to obtain their viewpoints about potential effects of these regulations. For example, we interviewed officials from the Consumer Financial Protection Bureau (CFPB), Department of Housing and Urban Development (HUD), Department of the Treasury's Office of Financial Research, Federal Deposit Insurance Corporation (FDIC), Federal Housing Finance Agency (FHFA), Board of Governors of the Federal Reserve System (Federal Reserve), Financial Stability Oversight Council, Office of the Comptroller of the Currency (OCC), and Securities and Exchange Commission (SEC). Stakeholders and others we interviewed included credit rating agencies; groups representing mortgage lenders, securitizers, and investors; groups representing consumer interests; and academics. We chose these groups and individuals because they had a range of views.

## Agencies' Plans to Monitor and Assess the Effects of the QM and QRM Provisions

To examine the extent to which agencies have plans in place to monitor and assess the effects of the QM and QRM provisions on the residential mortgage market, we identified and reviewed requirements and guidance relating to agencies' efforts to monitor and assess regulations (criteria). Specifically, we reviewed provisions of the Dodd-Frank Wall Street Reform and Consumer Protection Act (Dodd-Frank Act) that requires CFPB to assess its significant rules and publish a report of its assessment.[101] We also identified and reviewed Executive Orders related to agencies' efforts to conduct retrospective reviews.[102] Moreover, we identified and reviewed Office of Management and Budget (OMB) memorandums associated with these Executive Orders.[103] Finally, we reviewed prior GAO reports that examined agencies efforts to conduct retrospective reviews of regulations.[104]

To examine efforts and plans to monitor and assess the effects of the QM and QRM regulations, we focused our review on the retrospective review activities of CFPB, HUD, and the six agencies responsible for the QRM regulations—FDIC, FHFA, Federal Reserve, HUD, OCC, and SEC. We did not evaluate the efforts of the Departments of Agriculture and Veterans Affairs to review their QM regulations because they had not promulgated their own rules when we began our analysis and because their programs represent a smaller portion of the residential mortgage market. To understand federal agencies' efforts and plans to monitor and assess the effects of the QM and

QRM regulations, we reviewed *Federal Register* releases and other agency documents pertaining to retrospective reviews. For example, we identified and reviewed agency publications that contained plans to conduct retrospective reviews of the QM and QRM regulations, such as CFPB's 2013 and 2014 strategic plans, as well as HUD's final QM regulations, its 2014 and 2015 retrospective review plan, and its 2014-2018 strategic plan. During our review, we also examined CFPB's efforts to expand reporting requirements for Home Mortgage Disclosure Act (HMDA) data and examined the extent to which the expanded reporting might include data useful to monitor and assess the QM and QRM regulations. For example, we reviewed CFPB's 2014 proposed rule to expand HMDA reporting. Similarly, we reviewed FHFA's efforts to develop a National Mortgage Database and the extent to which it may include data to monitor and assess the QM and QRM regulations. We also interviewed federal agency officials (from CFPB, FDIC, FHFA, Federal Reserve, HUD, OCC, and SEC) about their plans to conduct retrospective reviews of the QM and QRM regulations.

We conducted this performance audit from November 2013 to June 2015 in accordance with generally accepted government auditing standards. Those standards require that we plan and perform the audit to obtain sufficient, appropriate evidence to provide a reasonable basis for our findings and conclusions based on our audit objectives. We believe that the evidence obtained provides a reasonable basis for our findings and conclusions based on our audit objectives.

## APPENDIX II: LIST OF STUDIES REVIEWED

American Bankers Association. *21st Annual ABA Real Estate Lending Survey Report.* Washington, D.C.: 2014.

Ashworth, Roger, Laurie Goodman, Brian Landy, and Lidan Yang. "The Coming Crisis in Credit Availability." *Amherst Mortgage Insight.* May 30, 2012.

Bai, Bing. Board of Governors of the Federal Reserve System. *July 2014 Senior Loan Officer Opinion Survey on Bank Lending Practices.* Washington, D.C.: August 4, 2014.

Board of Governors of the Federal Reserve System. *Changes in U.S. Family Finances from 2007 to 2010: Evidence from the Survey of Consumer Finances.* Washington, D.C.: June 2012. Board of Governors of the

Federal Reserve System. *Report to the Congress on Risk Retention.* Washington, D.C.: October 2010.

Bureau of Consumer Finance Protection. *Ability-to-Repay and Qualified Mortgage Standards under the Truth in Lending Act.* Washington, D.C.: January 2013.

Coalition for Sensible Housing Policy. *Updated QRM Proposal Strikes Balance: Preserves Access While Safeguarding Consumers and the Markets.* Washington, D.C.: October 24, 2013.

DBRS. A*ssessing U.S. RMBS Pools under the Ability-to-Repay Rules.* New York, N.Y.: May 2014.

Department of Housing and Urban Development. *Economic Analysis Statement: Qualified Mortgage Definition for Insured or Guaranteed Single Family Mortgages.* Washington, D.C.: November 2013.

Department of Housing and Urban Development. *Economic Analysis Statement: Qualified Mortgage Definition for Insured or Guaranteed Single Family Mortgages.* Washington, D.C.: (undated).

Federal Housing Finance Agency. "Qualified Residential Mortgages." *Mortgage Market Note*, 11-02. Washington, D.C.: April 11, 2011.

Fitch Ratings. *U.S. RMBS Qualified and Nonqualified Mortgage Criteria.* New York, N.Y.: March 2014.

Goldman Sachs. "Assessing the Impact of QM." *The Mortgage Analyst.* New York, N.Y.: October 10, 2013.

Moody's Analytics. *Moody's Approach to Assessing Incremental Risk Posed by the Ability-to-Repay Rules in U.S. RMBS.* New York, N.Y.: March 25, 2014.

Moody's Analytics. *Cost of Housing Finance Reform.* New York, N.Y.: November 2013.

Mortgage Bankers Association. *MBA Comment on Reopened Comment Period for QM Rule.* Washington, D.C.: July 9, 2012.

Office of Financial Research. *2013 Annual Report.* Washington, D.C.: December 2013.

Quercia, Roberto G., Lei Ding, and Carolina Reid. *Balancing Risk and Access: Underwriting Standards and Qualified Residential Mortgages.* Chapel Hill, N.C.: Center for Community Capital at the University of North Carolina, and Center for Responsible Lending, January 2012.

Reid, Carolina, and Roberto G. Quercia. *Risk, Access, and the QRM Reproposal.* Chapel, Hill, N.C.: Center for Community Capital at the University of North Carolina, September 2013.

Schwartz, Faith A., Margarita S. Brose, and Stuart I. Quinn. *QRM and Risk Retention Standards: Foundations for a Sound Housing Market.* Irvine, Calif.: Corelogic, December 2013.

Schwartz, Faith A. and Margarita S. Brose. *ATR/QM Standards: Foundations for a Sound Housing Market.* New York, N.Y.: CoreLogic, February 12, 2013.

Seidman, Ellen, Jun Zhu, and Laurie Goodman. "QRM, Alternative QRM: Loan Default Rates." *Urban Wire: Housing and Housing Finance.* Washington, D.C.: Urban Institute, October 17, 2013.

Seidman, Ellen, Jun Zhu, and Laurie Goodman. "QRM vs. Alternative QRM: Quantifying the Comparison." *Urban Wire: Housing and Housing Finance.* Washington, D.C.: Urban Institute, October 7, 2013.

Standard and Poor's. *Methodology and Assumptions for Adjusting RMBS Loss Severity Calculations for Loans Covered under Ability-to-Repay and Qualified Mortgage Standards.* New York, N.Y.: January 23, 2014.

The Center for Responsible Lending, Consumer Federation of America, and The Leadership Council on Civil and Human Rights. *Request for Comment on Qualified Mortgage.* Durham, N.C.: July 9, 2012.

White, Joshua, and Scott Bauguess. *Qualified Residential Mortgage: Background Data Analysis on Credit Risk Retention.* Washington, D.C.: Securities and Exchange Commission (Division of Economic and Risk Analysis), August 2013.

## End Notes

[1] See Mark Zandi and Cristian deRitis, *The Road to Reform* (Moody's Analytics: September 2013). Realized loss is the amount unrecovered from the sale of a foreclosed mortgage loan or real estate-owned property. It is equal to the amount of the outstanding principal balance of the loan, all unpaid scheduled interest, and all fees applied to the sale of the property minus the amount received from liquidation.

[2] Pub. L. No. 111 -203, 124 Stat. 1376 (2010).

[3] 78 Fed. Reg. 6408 (Jan. 30, 2013). CFPB issued additional final rules to amend and clarify the provisions of the January 2013 final rule: 78 Fed. Reg. 35430 (June 12, 2013); 78 Fed. Reg.44686, (July 24, 2013); 78 Fed. Reg. 60382 (Oct. 1, 2013); 78 Fed. Reg. 62993 (Oct. 23, 2013); and 79 Fed. Reg. 65300 (Nov. 3, 2014).

[4] The Dodd-Frank Act defines a securitizer as an issuer of an asset-backed security or a person who organizes and initiates an asset-backed securities transaction by selling or transferring assets, either directly or indirectly, including through an affiliate, to the issuer.

[5] 79 Fed. Reg. 77602 (Dec. 24, 2014). The six agencies responsible for the risk-retention rule are the Federal Deposit Insurance Corporation, Federal Housing Finance Agency, Board of Governors of the Federal Reserve System, Department of Housing and Urban Development, Office of the Comptroller of the Currency, and the Securities and Exchange Commission.

[6] See appendix II for a list of the studies we reviewed. We identified these analyses through means that included consultation with subject-matter experts, electronic searches of scholarly databases, and examination of studies conducted by agencies to inform the rulemakings. In some cases, we identified limitations in individual studies, which we mention when reporting on their specific findings later in this report.

[7] There is no uniform definition of default across the lending industry. For purposes of this report, we use the definition provided above.

[8] Financial institutions include the enterprises, private institutions approved by Ginnie Mae, and other private institutions that issue securities under their own authority.

[9] The Housing and Economic Recovery Act of 2008 established FHFA and gave the agency the authority to place Fannie Mae and Freddie Mac into conservatorship. Fannie Mae and Freddie Mac were placed into conservatorship on September 6, 2008.

[10] Before the housing crisis, the enterprises also invested in nontraditional mortgages such as subprime and Alt-A mortgages, which were higher-risk investments.

[11] Real estate investment trusts own income-producing real estate and in some cases engage in financing real estate. For a more information on the secondary market and the role of securitization, see GAO, *Housing Finance System: A Framework for Assessing Potential Changes*, GAO-15-131 (Washington, D.C.: Oct. 7, 2014).

[12] Simultaneous loan means another consumer credit transaction or certain home equity transaction that will be secured by the same dwelling and made to same consumer. 15 U.S.C. § 1639c(a)(2); 12 C.F.R. § 1026.43(b)(12).

[13] The monthly debt-to-income ratio represents the percentage of a borrower's total monthly income that goes toward total monthly debt obligations, including the mortgage payments, simultaneous loans, mortgage-related obligations, current debt obligations, alimony, and child support. A higher ratio is generally associated with a higher risk that the borrower will have cash flow problems and may miss mortgage payments. The creditor can determine the appropriate ratio.

[14] Small creditors are defined as those that issue no more than 500 first lien mortgages per year and have assets of $2 billion annually (adjusted for inflation). In February 2015, CFPB issued proposed regulations that would raise the loan origination limit for determining eligibility for small-creditor status from 500 originations secured by a first lien to 2,000 originations. 80 Fed. Reg. 7770 (Feb. 11, 2015).

[15] This category is designated as temporary because it applies only as long as Fannie Mae and Freddie Mac remain in federal conservatorship or until January 10, 2021, whichever comes first. For the federal agencies, the category applies until an agency's own QM regulations take effect or until January 10, 2021, whichever comes first. HUD issued final QM regulations, which became effective in January 2014. VA issued interim final regulations in May 2014, which became effective immediately. USDA's Rural Housing Service issued proposed QM regulations in March 2015.

[16] A final rule issued in June 2013 provided a 2-year transition period during which small creditors that do not operate predominately in rural or underserved areas can offer balloon payment QMs if they hold the loans in portfolio.

[17] 12 C.F.R § 1026.43(e)(1). A conclusive presumption is a "presumption that cannot be overcome by any additional evidence or argument," according to *Black's Law Dictionary* (9th ed. 2009).

[18] 79 Fed. Reg. 77602 (Dec. 24, 2014).

[19] Pub. L. No.111-203, §1022(d) (codified at 12 U.S.C. §5512(d)).

[20] Executive Order 13563; Office of Management and Budget Memorandums M-11-10, 11-19, and 11-25; Executive Order 13579; Office of Management and Budget Memorandum 11-28; and Executive Order 13610.

[21] Office of Management and Budget Memorandums M-11-19, M-11-25, and M-11-28.

[22] Office of Management and Budget Memorandums M-11-10 and M-11-28.

[23] Cash-out refinances occur when borrowers convert their home equity into cash for personal use, which increases the riskiness of the loan as the borrower has less equity in the home. For additional information describing the magnitude of nonprime refinance cash-out loans, see GAO, *Characteristics and Performance of Nonprime Mortgages*, GAO-09-848R (Washington, D.C.: July 28, 2009).

[24] As part of monetary policy, the Federal Reserve, through the Federal Open Market Committee, sets the federal funds rate at a level it believes will foster financial and monetary conditions consistent with achieving its monetary policy objectives, and it adjusts that target in line with evolving economic developments.

[25] The $1.25 trillion was the combined total of purchases under programs announced in November 2008 and March 2009. The Federal Reserve also announced a program in September 2012 that involved purchasing $40 billion in agency mortgage-backed securities purchases per month. That program was completed in October 2014. The Federal Reserve continues to re-invest the principal prepayments from its mortgage- backed securities portfolio. This policy is intended to help maintain accommodative financial conditions.

[26] The Federal Reserve defines the federal funds rate as the rate at which depository institutions trade balances at the Federal Reserve. Between 2004 and 2006, the Federal Reserve increased the federal funds rate by 4 percentage points, which contributed to increased mortgage rates.

[27] GAO, *Housing: Information on Recent Default and Foreclosure Trends for Home Mortgages and Associated Economic and Market Developments*, GAO-08-78R (Washington, D.C.: Oct. 16, 2007); and GAO-09-848R.

[28] GAO-09-848R.

[29] According to Federal Reserve staff, the rise in the conforming loan limit likely contributed to the share of jumbo loans reaching a low in 2009.

[30] GAO-09-848R.

[31] For example, see GAO-09-848R and Christopher J. Mayer, Karen M. Pence, and Shane M. Sherlund, *The Rise in Mortgage Defaults*, staff working paper 2008-59 in the Federal Reserve Finance and Economics Discussion Series (Washington, D.C.: 2008).

[32] Credit scores are used as part of the general underwriting criteria for FHA and enterprise loans.

[33] We previously reported that from 2000 through 2007, the average debt-to-income ratio for the subprime market rose from 38.8 to 41.5 percent. See GAO-09-848R.

[34] Mark Fleming, "In Which Dimension Is Credit Constrained?: Comparing Multiple Credit Measures to Normal," *The Market Pulse*, vol. 3, no.1 (CoreLogic: Jan. 17, 2014).

[35] FHA provided the average loan-to-value ratio data.

[36] Piggyback loans can result in higher combined loan-to-value ratios—that is, a ratio that takes the first mortgage and piggyback loans into account. However, we found in 2009 that combined loan-to-value ratio data do not capture all second liens. As a result, the average combined ratios presented likely are lower than the actual averages. For more information, see GAO-09-848R, p.9.

[37] Private-label mortgage-backed securities were a small part of the market before 2000.

[38] For additional information on market developments since 2000 and the federal role in the single-family housing finance system, see GAO-15-131.

[39] We reviewed 24 studies, but not all 24 studies directly examined the availability of QM loans. The studies also examined costs associated with the QM and QRM proposals as well as other factors not directly related to the QM regulations, such as the effects of credit scores on the availability of mortgage credit.

[40] See appendix II for a list of the studies we reviewed.

[41] GAO, *Mortgage Reform: Potential Impacts of Provisions in the Dodd-Frank Act on Homebuyers and the Mortgage Market*, GAO-11-656 (Washington, D.C.: July 19, 2011). This report examined QM criteria including negative amortization, loan term, balloon payments, and debt service-to-income ratio. Between 2001 and 2010, the percentage of loans that did not have negative amortization features ranged from 93.4 to 100 percent. The

percentage of loans with loan terms of 30 years or less ranged from 94.1 to 99.8 percent. The percentage of loans without balloon payments ranged from 97.7 to 100 percent. The percentage of loans that had debt-to-income ratios of 41 percent or less ranged from 58.3 to 75.2 percent. We were not able to assess all the effects of all the QM criteria due to data limitations, among other things.

[42] The Federal Reserve estimated that 14 percent of Fannie Mae and Freddie Mac refinance mortgages in 2010 had debt-to-income ratios above 43 percent. In comparison, the Federal Reserve estimated that 25 percent of Fannie Mae and Freddie Mac purchase mortgages and 31 percent of Fannie Mae and Freddie Mac refinance mortgages in 2006 had debt-to-income ratios above 43 percent. Board of Governors of the Federal Reserve System,*Mortgage Market Conditions and Borrower Outcomes: Evidence from the 2012 Data and Matched HMDA-Credit Report Data*, Federal Reserve Bulletin vol. 99, no. 4 (Washington, D.C.: November 2013).

[43] Center for Responsible Lending, Consumer Federation of America, and The Leadership Conference on Civil and Human Rights, *Request for Comment on Qualified Mortgage,* Docket Number: CFPB-2012-022 (Durham, N.C.: July 9, 2012).

[44] Due to data limitations, the researchers were not able to identify the entire universe of QM loans.

[45] Roberto G. Quercia, Lei Ding, and Carolina Reid, *Balancing Risk and Access: Underwriting Standards and Qualified Residential Mortgages* (Chapel Hill, N.C.: Center for Community Capital at the University of North Carolina, and Center for Responsible Lending, January 2012).

[46] Goldman Sachs, "Assessing the Impacts of QM," *The Mortgage Analyst* (New York, N.Y.: 2013). This analysis included loans sponsored or guaranteed by the enterprises, private-label securitizers, and FHA. The 29 percent figure was not included in the study but was provided to us by Goldman Sachs. Thus, 71 percent of the loans originated between 2005 and 2008 appeared to meet the QM standard and represented 53 percent of all defaults during that period.

[47] Thus, loans that appeared to meet the QM standard represented 75 percent of nondefaulting mortgages made from 2005 to 2008. The study's senior researcher noted that both the default estimate of 47 percent and the nondefault estimate of 25 percent understate the effect the QM regulations might have had on mortgage lending, because they were not able to identify three key QM features of QMs (that is debt-to-income, points and fees, and 5-year ARM indexed interest rates) due to data limitations. Had they been able to include these variables in their analyses, both of their estimates would have increased. It was not possible to estimate the magnitude of these increases.

[48] GAO, *Mortgage Financing: Actions Needed to Help FHA Manage Risks from New Mortgage Loan Products* GAO-05-194 (Washington, D.C.: Feb. 11, 2005); and *Nonprime Mortgages: Analysis of Loan Performance, Factors Associated with Defaults, and Data Sources*, GAO-10-805 (Washington, D.C.: Aug. 24, 2010); and GAO-08-78R.

[49] American Bankers Association, *21st Annual ABA Real Estate Lending Survey Report* (Washington, D.C.: 2014). The survey was sent to 2,600 banks and 208 responded. The majority of the respondents (76 percent) were small banks—those with assets of less than $1 billion.

[50] Targeted markets include restricted non-QM jumbo loans in high-cost markets, loans to borrowers with seasonal income such as farmers, and smaller-size loan markets in which many of the borrowers may not meet the QM definition.

[51] Board of Governors of the Federal Reserve System, *July 2014 Senior Loan Officer Opinion Survey on Bank Lending Practices* (Washington, D.C.: Aug. 4, 2014). The survey was based on responses from 75 domestic banks and 23 U.S. branches and agencies of foreign banks.

[52] This is the first time this survey included questions about the effect of the QM regulations.

[53] Board of Governors of the Federal Reserve System, *January 2015 Senior Loan Officer Opinion Survey on Bank Lending Practices* (Washington, D.C.: Feb. 2, 2015). This survey is based on 73 domestic banks and 23 U.S. branches and agencies of foreign banks.

[54] Bing Bai, "Data Show Surprisingly Little Impact of New Mortgage Rules," *Urban Wire: Housing and Housing Finance* (Washington, D.C.: Urban Institute, Aug. 21, 2014).

[55] For higher-priced QM loans, lenders are presumed to have satisfied the ability-to-repay requirements. However, borrowers can rebut the presumption by trying to prove that the lender was aware of information at loan origination that the borrower would not have enough income left for living expenses after paying the mortgage and other debts.

[56] The four largest credit rating agencies (Standard and Poor's, Moody's, Fitch, and DBRS) each issued their own methodologies or criteria.

[57] 78 Fed. Reg. 6408, 6567 (Jan. 30, 2013).

[58] The lowest probability of litigation (5 percent) was estimated for high-priced QM loans in nonjudicial states (that is, states in which foreclosure is not required to be conducted through court proceedings). The highest probability of litigation (50 percent) was estimated for a non-QM in a judicial state.

[59] The lowest probability of borrower success (10 percent) was associated with high-priced QM loans and the highest probability of borrower success (75 percent) was estimated for non-QM loans.

[60] To generate this estimate, CFPB first estimated that the cost of non-QM mortgages would increase by 10 basis points (0.1 percent) of the loan amount as a result of the litigation probability. Assuming loans with a weighted average life of 4 years, this could add roughly 2.5 basis points (0.025 percentage points) to the rate of each loan. For example, if the increased costs were passed to a borrower with a $210,000 loan with a 7.0 percent interest rate, the interest rate for the loan would increase to 7.025 percent and the monthly payment would rise by roughly $3.50, according to CFPB.

[61] Fitch Ratings, *U.S. RMBS Qualified and Nonqualified Mortgage Criteria* (New York, N.Y.: March 2014). This estimate was a weighted average and was based on an AAA probability of default and loss severity scenario. Fitch also generated credit enhancement adjustments for judicial and nonjudicial states.

[62] Standard and Poor's, *Methodology and Assumptions for Adjusting Loss Severity Calculations for Loans Covered under Ability-to-Repay and Qualified Mortgage Standards* (New York, N.Y.: Jan. 23, 2014). The estimate of a 30 basis point adjustment for non-QM loans was not included in the publication but was provided to us by Standard and Poor's.

[63] Credit enhancement protects investors against taking a loss on their securities when losses occur in the underlying asset pool. Credit enhancements are used to offset both potential loan losses and legal challenges. Credit enhancement can be structured in many different forms including securities subordination, excess interest rate spreads, cash reserves, and over-collateralization, among other things.

[64] GAO, *Bank Capital Reforms: Initial Effects of Basel III on Capital, Credit, and International Competitiveness*, GAO-15-67 (Washington, D.C.: Nov. 20, 2014).

[65] Board of Governors of the Federal Reserve, transcript of open Board meeting of October 22, 2014.

[66] 79 Fed. Reg. 77749(§_.8) (Dec. 24, 2014) and 79 Fed. Reg. 77761 (§_.19(b)(1)) (Dec. 24, 2014).

[67] The temporary QM exemption expires when conservatorship ends or January 10, 2021, whichever is sooner.

[68] The agencies contemplated alternate standards for QRM loans. For example, the risk- retention rule proposed in 2011 included a minimum loan-to-value ratio and borrower credit history restrictions. Federal agencies responsible for the QRM regulations and others examined the potential effect of making QRM standards more stringent. For example, an FHFA study analyzed a threshold of 80 percent for loan-to-value ratio and found that 30 percent of loans originated and acquired by the enterprises in 2009 would have met this threshold.

[69] Asset-Backed Securities Disclosure and Registration; Final Rule, 79 Fed. Reg. 57184 (Sept. 24, 2014).

[70] GAO-11-656.

[71] For example, see GAO-11-656; Joshua White and Scott Bauguess, *Qualified Residential Mortgage: Background Data Analysis on Credit Risk Retention* (Washington, D.C.: Securities and Exchange Commission, August 2013); and *Balancing Risk and Access: Underwriting Standards and Qualified Residential Mortgages.*

[72] For example, market participants told us that the available debt-to-income data for certain loan products such as low- and no-documentation loans likely were unreliable because income may have been misstated on these products.

[73] See 12 CFR §§ 1024.30-.41.

[74] For additional information, see GAO-15-131.

[75] GAO-15-131.

[76] Our analysis does not include a review of VA's assessment efforts for the QM regulations because the agency's rule had not been promulgated when we began our review. VA finalized its QM rule in May 2014. See 79 FR 26620 (May 9, 2014). USDA issued proposed QM regulations in March 2015.

[77] Executive Order 13579 (July 11, 2011) encourages independent regulatory agencies to comply with Executive Order 13563 (Jan.18, 2011). CFPB officials noted that although CFPB is not required to follow Executive Order 13579, they plan to follow the executive order in principle and spirit.

[78] HMDA was implemented by the Federal Reserve's Regulation C. On July 21, 2011, the rule-writing authority of Regulation C was transferred to CFPB. HMDA regulations are intended to provide loan data that can be used to assist (1) in determining whether financial institutions are serving the housing needs of their communities; (2) public officials in distributing public-sector investments to attract private investment to areas where it is needed; and (3) in identifying possible discriminatory lending patterns. HMDA regulations apply to financial institutions (banks, savings associations, credit unions, and other mortgage lending institutions).

[79] The Dodd-Frank Act §1094 requires CFPB to update HMDA to include the length of the loan; total points and fees; the length of any teaser or introductory interest rates; and the applicant or borrower's age and credit score. See 12 USC 2803.

[80] CFPB published its proposal to expand HMDA reporting requirements in August 2014, and accepted comments on the proposal through October 29, 2014. As of January 2015, CFPB had not completed its review of the comments. 79 Fed. Reg. 51732 (Aug. 29 2014).

[81] See 79 Fed. Reg. 51811 (Aug. 29, 2014)

[82] As noted above, HMDA loan data are intended to help determine whether financial institutions have been serving the housing needs of their communities and are not intended to assist efforts to examine loan performance.

[83] According to CFPB and FHFA officials, the agencies have worked together to develop the specifications of the database, such as identifying data elements. CFPB has provided financial support to create the database and FHFA has developed the infrastructure and hardware for NMDB.

[84] CoreLogic and BlackBox LLC are private vendors that provide residential mortgage loan-level data, among other things.

[85] Office of Management and Budget Memorandums M-11-10, M-11-19, M-11-25, and M-11-28. These memorandums identify best practices for conducting retrospective reviews of regulations.

[86] M-11-28 and Office of Management and Budget's Circular A-4: Regulatory Analysis, September 17, 2003.

[87] M-11-19 and M-11-25.

[88] See GAO, *Reexamining Regulations: Opportunities Exist to Improve Effectiveness and Transparency of Retrospective Reviews,* GAO-07-791 (Washington, D.C.: July 16, 2007).

[89] P.L. 111-203. Sec. 1400(c). See Pub. L. No. 111-203, §1062 for the requirement that the Secretary of the Treasury designate a date for the transfer of responsibility, among others, for promulgating regulations under various federal consumer financial laws to CFPB. See 75 Fed. Reg. 57252 (Sept. 20, 2010) for Treasury's designation of July 21, 2011, as the transfer date.

[90] 78 Fed. Reg. 75228 (Dec. 11, 2013).

[91] Residual income refers to the net income remaining for family support after all debts and obligations, including the mortgage, have been paid. For example, VA's mortgage insurance program requires lenders to compare the balance available for family support to guidelines based on family size, loan amount, and geographic location. See GAO, *Federal Housing Administration: Analysis of Options for Modifying Its Products, Market Presence, and Powers,* GAO-13-682 (Washington, D.C.: Sept. 9, 2013).

[92] 79 Fed. Reg. 77689 (Dec. 24, 2014).

[93] The Mortgage Lender Sentiment Survey is a quarterly online survey among senior executives of Fannie Mae's leading institution partners. The survey covers industry topics such as credit standards, consumer mortgage demand, and mortgage execution. The monthly Mortgage Credit Availability Index is calculated using a borrower's credit score, loan type, and loan-to-value ratio, among other factors. The index is a summary measure that indicates the availability of credit at a point in time.

[94] M-11-28.

[95] See GAO, *Results-Oriented Government: Practices That Can Help Enhance and Sustain Collaboration among Federal Agencies*, GAO-06-15 (Washington, D.C.: Oct. 21, 2005); and *Housing Assistance: Opportunities Exist to Increase Collaboration and Consider Consolidation*, GAO-12-554 (Washington, D.C.: Aug. 16, 2012).

[96] CoreLogic is a private company that provides data, analytics, technology, and services related to the mortgage industry, among other things.

[97] Conventional loans are mortgages that are not insured or guaranteed by the federal government. Conforming loans meet the requirements for purchase or securitization by Fannie Mae and Freddie Mac. Jumbo loans are larger than the maximum eligible for purchase by Fannie Mae and Freddie Mac, not including Alt-A or subprime loans. Alt-A loans are made to prime-credit borrowers and have some combination of nontraditional documentation, nonstandard product structure, or more liberal underwriting. Subprime loans are made to those who have impaired credit. Government-insured or guaranteed are loans insured or guaranteed by the Department of Veterans' Affairs or the Federal Housing Administration. Fixed-rate mortgages have interest rates that do not change over the entire term of the loans. Adjustable-rate mortgages have interest rates that change periodically based on changes in a specified index.

[98] GAO, *Foreclosure Mitigation: Agencies Could Improve Effectiveness of Federal Efforts with Additional Data Collection and Analysis*, GAO-12-296 (Washington, D.C.: June 28, 2012); and *Mortgage Reform: Potential Impacts of Provisions in the Dodd-Frank Act on Homebuyers and the Mortgage Market*, GAO-11-656 (Washington, D.C.: July 19, 2011).

[99] GAO, *Housing Finance System: A Framework for Assessing Potential Changes*, GAO-15-131 (Washington, D.C.: Oct. 7, 2014).

[100] American Bankers Association, *21st Annual ABA Real Estate Lending Survey Report* (Washington, D.C.: 2014); Board of Governors of the Federal Reserve System, *July 2014 Senior Loan Officer Opinion Survey on Bank Lending Practices* (Washington, D.C.: Aug. 4, 2014); and Bing Bai, *Data Show Surprisingly Little Impact of New Mortgage Rules* (Washington, D.C.: Urban Institute, Aug. 21, 2014).

[101] Pub. L. No. 111 -203, § 1022(d), 124 Stat. 1376, 1984 (2010).

[102] Executive Order 12866, *Regulatory Planning and Review*; Executive Order 13563, *Improving Regulation and Regulatory Review*; Executive Order 13579, *Regulation and Independent Regulatory Agencies*; and Executive Order 13610, *Identifying and Reducing Regulatory Burden*.

[103] Office of Management and Budget Memorandum M-11-10 provides guidance on Executive Order 13563; M-11-19 provides guidance about retrospective analysis of existing significant regulations; M-11-25 provides guidance about finalizing plans for retrospective analysis of existing rules; and M-11-28 provides guidance on Executive Order 13579.

[104] See GAO-07-791; *Dodd-Frank Act Regulations: Implementation Could Benefit from Additional Analyses and Coordination*, GAO-12-151 (Washington, D.C.: Nov. 10, 2011); and *Reexamining Regulations: Agencies Often Made Regulatory Changes, but Could Strengthen Linkages to Performance Goals*, GAO-14-268 (Washington, D.C.: Apr. 11, 2014).

In: Qualified Mortgages
Editor: Brenda Mills
ISBN: 978-1-63484-559-5


*Chapter 2*

# ABILITY-TO-REPAY AND QUALIFIED MORTGAGE RULE: SMALL ENTITY COMPLIANCE GUIDE*

***Consumer Financial Protection Bureau***

## 1. INTRODUCTION

During the years preceding the mortgage crisis, too many mortgages were made to consumers without regard to the consumers' ability to repay the loans. Loose underwriting practices by some creditors – including failure to verify consumers' income or debts and qualifying consumers for mortgages based on "teaser" interest rates after which monthly payments would jump to unaffordable levels – contributed to a mortgage crisis that led to the nation's most serious recession since the Great Depression.

In response to this crisis, in 2008 the Board of Governors of the Federal Reserve System adopted a rule under the Truth in Lending Act prohibiting creditors from making higher-priced mortgage loans without assessing consumers' ability to repay the loans. Creditors have had to follow these requirements since October 2009.

In the 2010 Dodd-Frank Wall Street Reform and Consumer Protection Act (the Dodd-Frank Act), Congress adopted similar (but not identical) Ability-to-Repay (ATR) requirements for virtually all closed-end residential mortgage

* This is an edited, reformatted and augmented version of a guidance document issued by the Consumer Financial Protection Bureau, January 8, 2014.

loans. Congress also established a presumption of compliance with the ATR requirements for a certain category of mortgages, called Qualified Mortgages (QMs).

In January 2013, the Consumer Financial Protection Bureau adopted a rule that implements the ATR/QM provisions of the Dodd-Frank Act. In May, July, and October 2013, the Bureau issued rules amending certain provisions of the January 2013 rule. The ATR/QM rule is the subject of this guide.

This rule generally applies to closed-end consumer credit transactions that are secured by a dwelling for which you receive an application on or after January 10, 2014.

As you will see in reading this guide, the ATR rule describes the minimum standards you must use to determine that consumers have the ability to repay the mortgages they are extended.

While the ATR rule provides eight specific factors you must consider (including verifications of income or assets relied on, employment if relied on, and review of credit history), the rule does not dictate that you follow particular underwriting models.

The rule also contains special requirements for creditors that are refinancing their own customers into more affordable loans to help those customers avoid payment shock.

In addition to the general ATR requirements, the rule also defines the requirements for Qualified Mortgages and how QM status works if there is a question about whether a creditor has assessed the borrower's ATR.

The rule provides a safe harbor for QMs that are not higher-priced. Loans that are higher-priced and meet the definition of a Qualified Mortgage have a different protection, that of a rebuttable presumption that the creditor complied with the ATR requirements.

This guide explains the requirements for creditors to follow to determine whether the loans your organization originates meet the QM requirements and, if so, whether they will receive either a safe harbor or rebuttable presumption of compliance with the ATR requirements.

It also discusses the grounds for rebutting the presumption for higher-priced QMs – principally, that the consumer's income, debt obligations, and payments on the loan and any simultaneous loans – did not leave the consumer with sufficient residual income/assets left to live on.

Qualified Mortgages have three types of requirements: restrictions on loan features, points and fees, and underwriting. One of the underwriting requirements under the general definition for Qualified Mortgages is that the borrower's total debt-to-income ratio is not higher than 43 percent.

For a temporary, transitional period, certain loans that are eligible for sale or guarantee by a government-sponsored enterprise (GSE) – the Federal National Mortgage Association (Fannie Mae) or the Federal Home Loan Mortgage Corporation (Freddie Mac) – or are eligible under specified federal agencies' guarantee or insurance programs will be considered Qualified Mortgages under a temporary definition. The loans must meet certain QM restrictions on loan features and points and fees, but they are not subject to a flat 43 percent DTI limit.

In response to the special concerns of small creditors and to preserve access to nonconforming mortgages and mortgages in rural and underserved areas, there are also special provisions for Qualified Mortgages held in portfolio by small creditors, including some types of balloon-payment mortgages. These Qualified Mortgages have a different, higher threshold for when they are considered higher-priced for Qualified Mortgage purposes than other Qualified Mortgages. They also are not subject to the 43 percent DTI limit.

Finally, the rule bans most prepayment penalties, except on certain non-higher-priced Qualified Mortgages with either fixed or step rates. Prepayment penalties are allowed on these non-higher- priced loans only if the penalties satisfy certain restrictions and are permitted under law and if the creditor has offered the consumer an alternative loan without such penalties.

## I. What Is the Purpose of this Guide?

The purpose of this guide is to provide an easy-to-use summary of the ATR/QM rule. This guide also highlights issues that small creditors, and those that work with them, might find helpful to consider when implementing the rule.

This guide also meets the requirements of Section 212 of the Small Business Regulatory Enforcement Fairness Act of 1996, which requires the Bureau to issue a small-entity compliance guide to help small businesses comply with these new regulations.

Although underwriting standards and verification practices have tightened considerably since the financial crisis, creditors may want to review their processes, underwriting guidelines, software, contracts, or other aspects of their business operations in order to identify any changes needed to comply with this rule.

Changes related to this rule may take careful planning, time, or resources to implement. This guide will help you identify and plan for any necessary changes.

To support rule implementation and ensure the industry is ready for the new consumer protections, the Bureau will coordinate with other agencies, publish plain-anguage guides, publish updates to the Official Interpretations, and publish readiness guides.

The guide summarizes the ATR/QM rule, but it is not a substitute for the rule. Only the rule and its Official Interpretations (also known as Commentary) can provide complete and definitive information regarding its requirements. The discussions below provide citations to the sections of the rule on the subject being discussed. Keep in mind that the Official Interpretations, which provide detailed explanations of many of the rule's requirements, are found after the text of the rule and its appendices. The interpretations are arranged by rule section and paragraph for ease of use. The complete rule, as issued on January 10, 2013 and the Official Interpretations are available at http://www.consumerfinance.gov/regulations/Ability-To-Repay-and-qualified-mortgage-standards-under-the-truth-in-lending-act-regulation-z/. Additionally, CFPB issued three final rules to amend and clarify provisions in the January 2013 Final Rule: the June 2013 ATR/QM Concurrent Final Rule, July 2013 Final Rule, and the October 2013 Final Rule.

The focus of this guide is the ATR/QM rule. This guide does not discuss other federal or state laws that may apply to the origination of closed-end credit.

At the end of this guide, there is more information about the rule and related implementation support from the Bureau.

## II. Who Should Read this Guide?

If your organization originates closed-end residential mortgage loans, you may find this guide helpful. This guide will help you determine your compliance obligations for the mortgage loans you originate.

This guide may also be helpful to secondary market participants, software providers, and other companies that serve as business partners to creditors.

## III. Who Can I Contact about this Guide or the ATR/QM Rule?

If, after reviewing this guide and the regulation(s) and commentary it addresses, you have a question regarding regulatory interpretation, please email CFPB_reginquiries@cfpb.gov with your specific question, including reference to the applicable regulation section(s). If you do not have access to the internet, you may leave this information in a voicemail at 202-435-7700.

Email comments about the guide to CFPB_ MortgageRules Implementation@cfpb.gov Your feedback is crucial to making this guide as helpful as possible. The Bureau welcomes your suggestions for improvements and your thoughts on its usefulness and readability.

The Bureau is particularly interested in feedback relating to:

- How useful you found this guide for understanding the rule
- How useful you found this guide for implementing the rule at your business
- Suggestions you have for improving the guide, such as additional implementation tips

# 2. Overview of the Ability-to-Repay/Qualified Mortgage Rule

## I. What Is the ATR/QM Rule about?

The ATR/QM rule requires that you make a reasonable, good-faith determination before or when you consummate a mortgage loan that the consumer has a reasonable ability to repay the loan, considering such factors as the consumer's income or assets and employment status (if relied on) against:

- The mortgage loan payment
- Ongoing expenses related to the mortgage loan or the property that secures it, such as property taxes and insurance you require the consumer to buy
- Payments on simultaneous loans that are secured by the same property
- Other debt obligations, alimony, and child-support payments

The rule also requires you to consider and verify the consumer's credit history.

As discussed in more detail below, the rule provides a presumption that you have complied with the ATR rule if you originate QMs.

QMs generally cannot contain certain risky features (such as allowing interest-only payments or negative amortization). In addition, points and fees on QMs are limited. For a loan to be a QM, it also must meet certain underwriting criteria.

In exchange for meeting these requirements, QMs receive either a conclusive or a rebuttable presumption that you, the creditor, complied with the ATR requirements. The type of presumption depends on the pricing of the loan - whether the loan is not higher-priced or is higher priced.

The ATR/QM rule also implements other provisions of the Dodd-Frank Act that:

- Limit prepayment penalties
- Require that you retain records for three years after consummation showing you complied with ATR and other provisions of this rule

## II. When Do I have to Start following this Rule ?

This rule applies to transactions covered under the rule for which you receive an application on or after January 10, 2014.

## III. What Transactions Are Covered by the ATR/QM Rule? (§ 1026.43(a))

The Bureau's ATR/QM rule applies to almost all closed-end consumer credit transactions secured by a dwelling including any real property attached to the dwelling. This means loans made to consumers and secured by residential structures that contain one to four units, including condominiums and co-ops. Unlike some other mortgage rules, the ATR/QM rule is not limited to first liens or to loans on primary residences.

However, some specific categories of loans are excluded from the rule. Specifically, the rule **does not apply to:**

- Open-end credit plans (home equity lines of credit, or HELOCs)
- Time-share plans
- Reverse mortgages
- Temporary or bridge loans with terms of 12 months or less (with possible renewal)
- A construction phase of 12 months or less (with possible renewal) of a construction-to- permanent loan
- Consumer credit transactions secured by vacant land

In addition, certain types of creditors or loan programs may be exempt from the ATR requirements. (*See "Which types of creditors and loan programs are exempt from the ability-to-repay requirements?"*)

**Implementation Tip:** The Truth in Lending Act applies to a loan modification only if it is considered a refinancing under Regulation Z. If a loan modification is not subject to the Truth in Lending Act, it is not subject to the ATR/QM rule. Therefore, you should determine if a loan modification is a refinancing to see if the ATR/QM rule applies. You will find the rules for determining whether a loan workout is a modification or a refinance in Regulation Z at § 1026.20(a) and accompanying Commentary.

## IV. How Long Do I have to Keep Records on Compliance with the ATR/QM Rule? (§ 1026.25(c)(3))

The rule requires that you retain evidence that you complied with the ATR/QM rule, including the prepayment penalty limitations, for three years after consummation, though you may want to keep records longer for business purposes.

# 3. About Ability to Repay

## I. What Is the General ATR Standard? (Comment 1026.43(c)(1)- 2)

Under the general ATR standard, you must make a reasonable, good-faith determination before or when you consummate a covered mortgage loan that the consumer has a reasonable ability to repay the loan.

## II. What Are the Eight ATR Underwriting Factors I must Consider and Verify under the Rule? (Comment 102 6.43 (c)(2) - 4)

A reasonable, good-faith ATR evaluation must include eight ATR underwriting factors:

1. Current or reasonably expected income or assets (other than the value of the property that secures the loan) that the consumer will rely on to repay the loan
2. Current employment status (if you rely on employment income when assessing the consumer's ability to repay)
3. Monthly mortgage payment for this loan. You calculate this using the introductory or fully-indexed rate, whichever is higher, and monthly, fully-amortizing payments that are substantially equal (*See "What do I include on the debt side of the debt-to-income ratio when determining ATR?" for special rules for calculating payments for interest-only, negative-amortization, and balloon loans.*)
4. Monthly payment on any simultaneous loans secured by the same property
5. Monthly payments for property taxes and insurance that you require the consumer to buy, and certain other costs related to the property such as homeowners association fees or ground rent
6. Debts, alimony, and child- support obligations
7. Monthly debt-to-income ratio or residual income, that you calculated using the total of all of the mortgage and non-mortgage obligations listed above, as a ratio of gross monthly income
8. Credit history

**Implementation Tip:** You may already have underwriting policies, procedures, and internal controls that consider these factors. However, you should check your policies and procedures to ensure that they reflect that you will consider each of the eight factors. It may also be helpful to document how you consider the factors. However, the rule does not require validation of underwriting criteria using mathematical models.

The rule does not preclude you from considering additional factors, but you must consider at least these eight factors.

## III. How Do I Verify Information I Considered Using Reliable Third-Party Records? (Comment 1026.43(c)(3)- 4)

Your organization must verify the information you rely on using reasonably reliable third-party records. For example, you generally cannot rely on what consumers orally tell you about their income. You must verify a consumer's income using documents such as W-2s or payroll statements.

While you must follow the reasonably reliable third-party standard, the rule provides for a wide variety of sources that may help you to verify the information you rely on to determine ATR.

There are a wide variety of documents and sources of information your organization can use as you determine ATR, and you have significant flexibility in how you verify each of the eight factors. For example:

- In addition to a W-2 or payroll statement, you may verify income using tax returns, bank statements, receipts from check-cashing or funds-transfer services, benefits-program documentation, or records from an employer. Copies of tax-return transcripts or payroll statements can be obtained directly from the consumer or from a service provider, and need not be obtained directly from a government agency or employer, as long as the records are reasonably reliable and specific to the individual consumer.
- If a consumer has more income than, in your reasonable and good-faith judgment, is needed to repay the loan, you do not have to verify the extra income. For example, if a consumer has both a full- time and a part-time job and you reasonably determine that income from the full-time job is enough for the consumer to be able to repay the loan, you do not have to verify income from the part-time job.

- You can document a consumer's employment status by calling the employer and getting oral verification, as long as you maintain a record of the information you received on the call.
- You can use a credit report to verify a consumer's debt obligations; you do not need to obtain individual statements for every debt.
- If a consumer does not have a credit history from a credit bureau, you can choose to verify credit history using documents that show nontraditional credit references, such as rental payment history or utility payments.

**Implementation Tip:** If your organization does not currently verify any of the ATR underwriting factors, plan to create new verification, quality-control, and compliance processes and to make any related system adjustments.

**Implementation Tip:** While you do not have to retain actual paper copies of documentation used in underwriting a transaction, you must be able to reproduce such records accurately. For example, if you use a consumer's W-2 tax form to verify income, you must be able to reproduce the form itself, not merely the income information that was contained in the form. Accordingly, you can obtain records transmitted electronically, such as via email or a secure external Internet link to access information, if you can retain or otherwise reproduce such records accurately during the three years you must retain ATR records. (Comment 43(b)(13)-1)

## IV. What Is a Reasonably Reliable Third-Party Record? (§1026.43(c)(3))

Here is a list of some of the types of reasonably reliable third-party records your organization may choose to use. Note, however, that this list is not all-inclusive:

- Records from government organizations such as a tax authority or local government
- Federal, state, or local government agency letters detailing the consumer's income, benefits, or entitlements

- Statements provided by a cooperative, condominium, or homeowners association
- A ground rent or lease agreement
- Credit reports
- Statements for student loans, auto loans, credit cards, or existing mortgages
- Court orders for alimony or child support
- Copies of the consumer's federal or state tax returns
- W-2 forms or other IRS forms for reporting wages or tax withholding
- Payroll statements
- Military leave and earnings statements
- Financial institution records, such as bank account statements or investment account statements reflecting the value of particular assets
- Records from the consumer's employer or a third party that obtained consumer-specific income information from the employer
- Check-cashing receipts
- Remittance-transfer receipts

**Implementation Tip:** When determining ATR, you have to verify only the income or assets used to qualify the consumer for the loan.

**Implementation Tip:** When the consumers' applications list debt that does not show up on their credit reports, you must consider that debt in assessing either the consumers' debt-to-income ratios or residual income, but you do not need to independently verify that debt.

## V. How Do I Determine ATR? (§ 1026.43(c)(1))

Your organization is responsible for developing and applying its own underwriting standards and making changes to those standards over time in response to empirical information and changing economic and other conditions.

To help your organization incorporate the ATR concepts into its operations, the Bureau has prepared some examples that illustrate how your internal policies can influence your ATR determinations.

The list below is not a comprehensive list of all the ways your underwriting guidelines might measure ATR.

Each of you must look at the issue of ATR in the context of the facts and circumstances relevant to your market, your organization, and your individual consumers.

Given those caveats, here are some of the types of factors that may show that your **ATR determination was reasonable and in good faith**:

- Underwriting standards: You used standards to underwrite the transaction that have historically resulted in comparatively low rates of delinquency and default during adverse economic conditions.
- Payment history: The consumer paid on time for a significant time after origination or reset of an adjustable-rate mortgage.

Among the types of factors that may show that your ATR determination was not reasonable and in good faith:

- Underwriting standards: You ignored evidence that your underwriting standards are not effective at determining consumers' repayment ability.
- Inconsistency: You applied underwriting standards inconsistently or used underwriting standards different from those you used for similar loans without having a reasonable justification.
- Payment history: The consumer defaults early in the loan, or shortly after the loan resets, without having experienced a significant financial challenge or life-altering event.

The reasonableness and good faith of your determination of ATR depends on the facts and circumstances relevant to the particular loan. For example, a particular ATR determination may be reasonable and in good faith even though the consumer defaulted shortly after consummation if, for example, the consumer experienced a sudden and unexpected loss of income.

If the records you review indicate there will be a change in the consumers' repayment ability after consummation (for example, they plan to retire and not obtain new employment, or they plan to transition from full-time to part-time work) you must consider that information. (Comment 43(c)(1)-2) However, you may not make inquiries or verifications prohibited by Regulation B. (Comment 43(c)(1)-3)

## VI. Do Loans or Iginated under the General ATR Standard have to Comply with a Debt-to-Income (DTI) Threshold? (§ 1026.43(c) (2)(vii))

The general ATR standard requires creditors to consider DTI or residual income, but does not contain specific DTI or residual income thresholds.

## VII. What Do I Include on the Income Side of the Debt-to-Income Ratio when Determining ATR?

You can include earned income (wages or salary); unearned income (interest and dividends); and other regular payments to the consumer such as alimony, child support, or government benefits. In all cases, the amounts you rely upon to determine ATR must be verified.

Once you have information about the consumers' income, you will use it, along with the consumers' debt information, to calculate the DTI ratio or residual income.

## VIII. How Do I Calculate, Consider, and Confirm Income, Assets, Employment, and Credit History?

When you are evaluating the consumer's employment history, credit history, and income or assets to determine ATR, you must verify only what is relied on to determine ATR.

If a consumer has a full-time job and a part-time job and uses only the income from the full-time job to pay the loan, you do not need to verify the income from the part-time job. If two or more consumers apply for a mortgage, you do not have to consider both incomes – unless both incomes are required to qualify for the loan and demonstrate ATR.

The same principles apply to a consumer's assets, too.

Income does not have to be full-time or salaried for you to consider it in your ATR determination. You can consider seasonal or bonus income. Remember that income relied on has to be verified using reasonably reliable third-party records.

For example, you could verify a Christmas tree farmer's seasonal income via tax returns showing that the farmer earned $50,000 a year during the past three Decembers and nothing else the rest of the year, and divide that $50,000 evenly across 12 months.

Future income can count toward ATR if you verify it using reasonably reliable third-party records. Suppose you have a consumer who accepts a job in March, but will not start until he graduates from school in May. If the employer will confirm the job offer and salary in writing, you can consider the future expected income in your ATR determination.

### *i. Consumer-supplied income documents (§ 1026.43(b)(13))*

Sometimes you may have to rely on the consumers' report of their own income. For example, a cattle rancher might give you an updated profit-and-loss statement for the current year to supplement his tax returns from prior years. These records are reasonably reliable third-party records to the extent that an appropriate third party has reviewed them. For example, if a third-party accountant prepared or reviewed the cattle rancher's profit-and-loss statement, then you can use the statement to verify the rancher's current income.

### *ii. Types of employment information (§ 1026.43(c)(3))*

You can consider and verify many types of employment to use in making your ATR determination, including:

- Full-time
- Part-time
- Seasonal
- Irregular
- Military
- Self-employment

Consider the characteristics of the consumer's type of employment. A wheat farmer has a different income stream than a store clerk.

You can verify the consumer's employment by calling the employer and obtaining oral verification, so long as you make a written record memorializing the verification.

### *iii. Sources of credit history information (§ 1026.43(c)(3)(iii))*

A credit report generally is considered a reasonably reliable third-party record for verification purposes.

While the rule requires that you examine credit history, it does not prescribe a particular type of credit history to consider or prescribe specifically how you should judge the information you receive. Your consideration of credit history must be reasonable in light of the facts and circumstances.

- Credit history might include information about:
- Number and age of credit lines
- Payment history
- Judgments
- Collections
- Bankruptcies
- Nontraditional credit references such as rental payment history or utility payments

If you know, or have a reason to know, that the information on a consumer's credit report is inaccurate, you can ignore it. For example, there might be a fraud alert or a dispute on the credit report, or the consumer may present other evidence that contradicts the credit report. In those cases, you may choose to disregard the inaccurate or disputed items.

If the consumer lists a debt obligation that does not show up on the credit report, you may accept the consumer's statement about the existence and amount of the obligation without further verification.

## I X. What Do I Include on the Debt Side of the Debt-to-Income Ratio when Determining ATR?

In assessing a consumer's ATR, four underwriting factors help you evaluate the consumer's debts. You will need to find out the consumer's total monthly payments for:

1. The loan you are underwriting
2. Any simultaneous loans secured by the same property
3. Mortgage-related obligations – property taxes; insurance required by the creditor; fees owed to a condominium, cooperative, or

homeowners association; ground rent or leasehold payments; and special assessments

4. Current debt obligations, alimony, and child support

Once you have the total debt figure, you will use it, along with the consumer's total monthly income, to calculate the monthly debt-to-income ratio or residual income.

**Include** ongoing, required monthly, quarterly, or annual debts of the consumer.

**Do not include** debts paid off at or before consummation.

## X. How Do I Calculate, Consi der, and Confirm Debt Information?

***i. Calculating payments under the ATR standard for the loan you are underwriting: (§ 1026.43(c)(5))***

**General rule:** If the interest rate on the loan can vary during the term of the loan, as with an adjustable-rate or step-rate mortgage, when you calculate the monthly payment the consumer will have to make for the new loan, you will usually use the greater of the fully-indexed rate or the introductory rate.

You must base your calculations on substantially equal monthly payments that would fully amortize the loan.

**Special rules:** However, there are also special rules and guidance provided for certain types of loans:

- For balloon loans, the calculation depends on whether the loan is a higher-priced loan. Higher-priced loans are generally defined as having an annual percentage rate (APR) that, as of the date the interest rate is set, exceeds the Average Prime Offer Rate (APOR) by 1.5 percentage points or more for first-lien loans and 3.5 percentage points or more for subordinate-lien loans. APOR is published weekly at https://www.ffiec.gov/ratespread.
- For non-higher-priced balloon loans: Use the maximum payment scheduled during the first five years after the first regular periodic payment comes due.

- For higher-priced balloon loans: Use the maximum payment in the payment schedule, including any balloon payment.
- For interest-only loans: Use the greater of the fully-indexed or introductory rate and equal, monthly payments of principal and interest that will repay the outstanding loan amount on the date the loan recasts over the remaining term of the loan.
- For negative-amortization loans: Calculate the maximum loan amount, which will include the potential added principal assuming the consumer makes the minimum required payments until the date the loan recasts. Use the greater of the fully-indexed or introductory rate and equal, monthly payments of principal and interest that will repay that maximum loan amount on the date the loan recasts over the remaining term of the loan.

To be substantially equal, no two monthly payments should vary by more than 1 percent. For loans paid quarterly or annually, convert the payments into monthly payments when you determine ATR.

***ii. Calculating payments for simultaneous loans secured by the same property: (§ 1026.43(c)(6))***

A simultaneous transaction, such as a piggy-back or silent second, can influence a consumer's ATR. A transaction that recently closed or will close around the same time as the mortgage you are originating may not show up on the consumer's credit report.

But if you know, or have reason to know, that there is going to be a simultaneous transaction around the time your transaction consummates, you need to consider the monthly payment on that transaction in accordance with the following requirements.

- For simultaneous transactions that are not HELOCs - Your ATR assessment should include a monthly payment on the simultaneous loan that is calculated using the appropriate calculation method for adjustable-rate mortgages, interest-only loans, or other categories discussed above, depending on what type of simultaneous loan is made.
- For simultaneous transactions that are HELOCs - Your ATR assessment should include a monthly payment on the simultaneous loan that is calculated based on the amount of credit to be drawn down at or before consummation of the main loan.

### *iii. Mortgage-related obligations: (§ 1026.43(c)(3)and comment 43(c)(3)-5)*

You can get records for the consumer's mortgage-related obligations from many sources including:

- Property taxes: government entities or the amount listed on the title report (if the source of the information was a local taxing authority)
- Cooperative, condominium, or homeowners associations: a billing statement from the association
- Levies and assessments: statement from the assessing entity (for example, a water district bill)
- Ground rent: the current ground rent agreement
- Lease payments: the existing lease agreement
- Other records: can be reasonably reliable if they come from a third party

### *iv. Other recurring debts: (§ 1026.43(c)(3) and comment 43(c)(3)-6)*

The rule requires you to consider a consumer's current debt obligations and any alimony or child support the consumer is required to pay.

Typical recurrent monthly **debts** include:

- Student loans
- Auto loans
- Revolving debt
- Existing mortgages not being paid off at or before consummation

You can generally verify such obligations based on the consumer's credit report or based on other items reported on the consumer's application. Creditors have significant flexibility to consider current debt obligations in light of facts and circumstances, including that an obligation is likely to be paid off soon after consummation. Similarly, creditors should consider whether debt obligations in forbearance or deferral at the time of underwriting are likely to affect the consumer's ability to pay after the expiration of the forbearance or deferral period. *(See discussion regarding when it is appropriate to disregard information in a credit report because it is disputed or inaccurate.)*

When two or more customers apply as joint obligors with primary liability on a loan, consider the debt obligations and credit histories of both of them in assessing their ability to repay the loan. But you do not have to include in your ATR consideration the debt obligations or credit history of someone who is merely a guarantor or surety on the loan. (Comment 43(c)(2)(vi)-2)

## XI. Does the ATR Rule Ban Certain Loan Features or Transaction Types? (§ 1026.43(c)(2) and (5))

The ATR rule does not ban any particular loan features or transaction types, but a particular loan to a particular consumer is not permissible if the creditor does not make a reasonable, good-faith determination that the consumer has the ability to repay. Thus, the rule helps ensure underwriting practices are reasonable.

For example, it will no longer be possible to originate loans based on stated income. You must now verify the consumer's income or assets and employment relied on in order to comply with the ATR rule.

Likewise, the rule also requires you to underwrite loans with nontraditional features, such as interest-only or negative-amortization periods, by considering the consumer's ability to repay the loan after the initial period.

For higher-priced balloon loans that do not meet the requirements of a balloon-payment QM, you will need to underwrite the balloon payment itself, though balloon loans that are not higher- priced do not have this requirement.

## XII. What Happens if a Consumer Has Trouble Repaying a Loan I Originate under the General ATR Rule? What Happens if My Organization Violates the Regulation?

Whether or not you complied with the ATR requirements is based on the information available during origination.

For example, you are not in violation of the ATR requirements if consumers cannot repay their mortgage loans solely because they experienced a sudden and unexpected job loss after you originated the loan. The ATR determination applies to information known at or before consummation.

However, if consumers have trouble repaying a loan you originate, they could claim that you failed to make a reasonable, good-faith determination of their ATR before you made the loan. If the consumers prove this claim in court, you could be liable for, among other things, up to three years of finance charges and fees the consumers paid as well as the consumers' legal fees.

There is a three-year statute of limitations on ATR claims brought as affirmative cases. After three years, consumers can bring ATR claims only as setoff/recoupment claims in a defense to foreclosure.

## XIII. Which Types of Creditors and Loan Programs Are Exempt from the Ability-to-Repay Requirements? (§ 1026.43(a)(3)(iv) to (vi))

Extensions of credit made by certain types of creditors are exempt from the ATR requirements.

- Extensions of credit made by creditors designated by the U.S. Department of the Treasury as Community Development Financial Institutions and creditors designated by HUD as either a Community Housing Development Organization or a Downpayment Assistance Provider of Secondary Financing are exempt from the ATR requirements, under certain conditions.
- Extensions of credit made by creditors designated as nonprofit organizations under section 501(c)(3) of the Internal Revenue Code of 1986 that extend credit no more than 200 times annually, provide credit only to low-to-moderate income consumers, and follow their own written procedures to determine that consumers have a reasonable ability to repay their loans are also generally exempt from the ATR requirements.

Extensions of credit made pursuant to certain loan programs are exempt from the ATR requirements.

- Extensions of credit made by housing finance agencies directly to consumers, as well as extensions of credit made by other creditors pursuant to a program administered by a housing finance agency, are exempt from the ATR requirements. This ATR exemption applies to extensions of credit made pursuant to a program administered by a housing finance agency, regardless of the funding source (e.g., Federal, State, or other sources).
- Extensions of credit made pursuant to an Emergency Economic Stabilization Act program, such as extensions of credit made pursuant

to a State Hardest Hit Fund program, are also exempt from the ATR requirements.

The exemptions above apply to all loans made by these creditors or pursuant to these loan programs, provided the conditions for the exemption are satisfied. An exempt loan remains exempt even if it is sold, assigned, or otherwise transferred to a creditor that would not qualify for the exemption.

Note that the ATR requirements do not apply to these loans. Thus, a loan that is eligible for one of these exemptions is not eligible for QM status, as the QM provisions are only applicable to loans subject to the ATR requirements. A consumer who obtained a loan that was exempt from the ATR requirements would have no ability-to-repay claim under the ATR/QM rule.

Please note that although these loans are not subject to the ATR requirements, they still are subject to the restrictions on prepayment penalties and may not be structured as open-end credit plans to evade those restrictions.

## 4. About Qualified Mortgages

### I. What Is a Qualified Mortgage? (§1026.43(e) and (f))

The rule provides a presumption that creditors that originate Qualified Mortgages (QMs) have complied with the ATR requirements. That means a court will treat a case differently if a consumer files an ATR claim where the loan is a QM. Creditors will be presumed to have complied with the ATR requirements if they issue QMs. The QM standard helps protect consumers from unduly risky mortgages. It also gives you more certainty about potential liability.

There are four types of Qualified Mortgages under the rule. Two types, the General and Temporary QM definitions, can be originated by all creditors. Two other types, Small Creditor and Balloon-Payment QMs, can only be originated by small creditors. (*See "Are there different types of QMs?"*)

The QM requirements generally focus on prohibiting certain risky features and practices, such as negative amortization and interest-only periods and loan terms longer than 30 years.

In addition, for all types of QMs, points and fees generally may not exceed 3 percent of the total loan amount, but higher thresholds are provided for loans below $100,000. (*See "What are the QM points-and-fees caps and what do I include when calculating points and fees?"*)

The type of presumption of compliance for a QM depends on whether it is **higher-priced**. Qualified Mortgages under the General and Temporary definitions are considered higher-priced if they have an APR that exceeds the APOR by 1.5 percentage points or more for first-lien loans and 3.5 percentage points or more for subordinate-lien loans. Small Creditor and Balloon-Payment QMs are considered higher-priced if they have an APR that exceeds the APOR by 3.5 percentage points or more for both first-lien and subordinate-lien loans. (*See "What makes a QM loan higher-priced?"*)

If a loan that is not **higher-priced** satisfies the QM criteria, a court will conclusively presume that you complied with the ATR rule.

If a **higher-priced** loan meets the QM criteria, a court will presume it complies with the ATR requirements, but the consumer may rebut the presumption.

## II. What Is the Difference between Safe Harbor and Rebuttable Presumption in Terms of Liability Protection? (§1026.43(e)(1))

QMs can receive two different levels of protection from liability. Which level they receive depends on whether the loan is higher-priced or not. (*See "What makes a QM loan higher-priced?"*)

### *i. Safe harbor*

QMs that **are not higher-priced** have a safe harbor, meaning that they are conclusively presumed to comply with the ATR requirements.

Under a **safe harbor**, if a court finds that a mortgage you originated was a QM, then that finding conclusively establishes that you complied with the ATR requirements when you originated the mortgage.

For example, a consumer could claim that in originating the mortgage you did not make a reasonable and good-faith determination of repayment ability and that you therefore violated the ATR rule. If a court finds that the loan met the QM requirements and was not higher-priced, the consumer would lose this claim.

The consumer could attempt to show that the loan is not a QM (for example, under the General QM definition that the DTI ratio was miscalculated and exceeds 43 percent), and therefore is not presumed to comply with the ATR requirements. However, if the loan is indeed a QM and is not higher-priced, the consumer has no recourse under this regulation.

***ii. Rebuttable presumption***

QMs that **are higher-priced** have a rebuttable presumption that they comply with the ATR requirements, but consumers can rebut that presumption.

Under a **rebuttable presumption**, if a court finds that a mortgage you originated was a higher- priced QM, a consumer can argue that you violated the ATR rule. However, to prevail on that argument, the consumer must show that based on the information available to you at the time the mortgage was made, the consumer did not have enough residual income left to meet living expenses after paying their mortgage and other debts.

The rebuttable presumption provides more legal protection and certainty to you than the general ATR requirements, but less protection and certainty than the safe harbor.

## III. What Makes a QM Loan Higher-Priced? (§ 1026.43(b)(4))

A Qualified Mortgage under the General or Temporary definition is **higher-priced** if:

- It is a first-lien mortgage for which, at the time the interest rate on the loan was set, the APR was 1.5 percentage points or more over the Average Prime Offer Rate (APOR).
- It is a subordinate-lien mortgage with an APR that, when the interest rate was set, exceeded the APOR by 3.5 percentage points or more.

For example, if the APOR is 5 percent at the time when the interest rate on a mortgage is set, then a first-lien mortgage is higher-priced if it has an APR of 6.5 percent or more.

A Small Creditor or Balloon-Payment QM is higher-priced if:

- It has an APR that, when the interest rate was set, exceeded the APOR by 3.5 percentage points or more, for both first- lien and subordinate-lien mortgages.

- For example, if the APOR is 5 percent at the time when the interest rate on a mortgage is set, a mortgage that is a Small Creditor Qualified Mortgage is higher- priced if it has an APR of 8.5 percent or more, regardless of whether it is first- or subordinate-lien loan.
- To calculate whether a loan's APR exceeds the APOR for a comparable loan by more than the relevant 1.5 or 3.5 percentage-point spread, you may use the rate- spread calculators and other guidance available online at http://www.ffiec.gov/ratespread/.

**Implementation Tip:** This special definition of higher-priced for Small Creditor and Balloon-Payment QMs only determines whether a loan has a safe harbor or rebuttable presumption of compliance with the ATR requirements. It does not affect whether a loan is a "higher-priced mortgage loan" (HPML) under other Bureau rules and does not exempt a loan from other requirements for HPMLs.

## IV. Are There Different Types of QMs?

There are four types of QMs. Two types of QMs, the General and Temporary QM definitions, can be originated by any creditor, regardless of the creditor's size. Two additional types of QMs, Small Creditor and Balloon-Payment QMs, can be originated only by small creditors.

For all four types, QMs that are higher-priced receive a rebuttable presumption and QMs that are not higher-priced receive safe harbor status. However, the definition of "higher-priced" is different for Small Creditor and Balloon-Payment QMs. (*See "What makes a QM loan higher priced?"*)

Some requirements are common across all four types of QM. These requirements include:

- A prohibition on negative amortization or interest-only payments
- A prohibition on loan terms in excess of 30 years
- Limitations on points and fees: The threshold is generally 3 percent of the loan balance, but larger amounts are allowed for loans under $100,000 (*See "What are the QM points-and- fees caps and what do I include when calculating points and fees?"*)

## V. What Types of QMs Can All Creditor Soriginate?

There are two types of Qualified Mortgage that all creditors are eligible to originate.

***i. Type 1: General QM definition (§ 1026.43(e)(2))***

General QM loans may not have negative-amortization, interest-only, or balloon-payment features or terms that exceed 30 years. They also may not have points and fees that exceed the specified limits.

**Implementation Tip:** Although consideration and verification of a consumer's credit history is not specifically incorporated into the General QM definition, you must verify a consumer's debt obligations using reasonably reliable third-party records, which may include use of a credit report or records that evidence nontraditional credit references.

In addition, in order for a loan to be a General QM loan, the creditor must:

- Underwrite based on a fully-amortizing schedule using the maximum rate permitted during the first five years after the date of the first periodic payment
- Consider and verify the consumer's income or assets, current debt obligations, alimony and child-support obbligations
- Determine that the consumer's total monthly debt-to-income ratio is no more than 43 percent, using the definitions and other requirements provided in appendix Q, which is derived from the Federal Housing Administration manual

**Implementation Tip:** When appendix Q does not resolve how a specific type of debt or income should be treated, creditors may rely on guidelines of the GSEs or certain federal agencies (listed below under "Temporary QM definition") to resolve the issue. However, a creditor may not rely on GSE or agency guidelines where such guidelines are in conflict with appendix Q standards.

***ii. Type 2: Temporary QM definition (§ 1026.43(e)(4))***

The rule also extends QM status to certain loans that are originated during a transitional period if they are eligible for purchase or guarantee by Fannie Mae or Freddie Mac (the government- sponsored enterprises (GSEs)) or for insurance or guarantee by certain federal agencies. Loans that receive QM status under the temporary provision will retain that status after the temporary provision expires, but new loans will not receive QM status after that date under the temporary provision. So, after expiration of the temporary provision, loans must meet the requirements for one of the other categories of Qualified Mortgages to be QMs.

The temporary provision expires, for loans eligible for purchase or guarantee by the GSEs, on the date that the GSEs exit federal conservatorship or receivership or on January 10, 2021, whichever occurs first.

The temporary provision for loans eligible for insurance or guarantee by specified federal agencies is a transition measure designed to give the agencies time to exercise separate authority under the Dodd-Frank Act to determine which of their loans will receive QM status. This temporary provision will expire on the date that the relevant agency's own QM rules take effect or on January 10, 2021, whichever occurs first.

Loans falling under the **Temporary QM definition** must meet the same requirements as General QM loans regarding prohibitions on risky features (negative-amortization, interest-only, and balloon-payment features), a maximum loan term of 30 years, and points-and-fees restrictions.

They must also meet at least **one** of these additional requirements:

- Eligible for purchase or guarantee by the Federal National Mortgage Association (Fannie Mae) or the Federal Home Loan Mortgage Corporation (Freddie Mac) while operating under federal conservatorship or receivership
- Eligible for Federal Housing Administration (FHA) insurance
- Eligible to be guaranteed by the U.S. Department of Veterans Affairs (VA)
- Eligible to be guaranteed by the U.S. Department of Agriculture (USDA)
- Eligible to be insured by the Rural Housing Service

Eligibility for purchase or guarantee by a GSE or insurance or guarantee by an agency can be established based on the following methods:

- Valid recommendation from a GSE Automated Underwriting System (AUS) or an AUS that relies on an agency underwriting tool
- GSE or agency guidelines contained in official manuals

- Written agreements between a GSE or agency and the creditor (or a direct sponsor or aggregator of the creditor)
- Individual loan waivers from a GSE or agency

To meet the Temporary QM definition, loans must be underwritten using the required guidelines of the entities above, including any relevant DTI guidelines. They do not have to meet the 43 percent debt-to-income ratio threshold that applies to General QM loans.

The creditor does not have to satisfy GSE or agency standards which are wholly unrelated to the credit risk or underwriting of the loan or any standards which apply after the consummation of the loan.

## VI. What Types of QMs Can Small Creditors Originate?

Small creditors can originate Qualified Mortgages under the General and Temporary QM definitions discussed above. In addition, there are two additional types of Qualified Mortgages that can only be originated by small creditors.

You can make these types of QMs only if you meet both of the following requirements:

- You had assets below $2 billion (to be adjusted annually for inflation by the Bureau) at the end of the last calendar year.
- You and your affiliates together originated no more than 500 first-lien, closed-end residential mortgages that are subject to the ATR requirements in the preceding calendar year.

An affiliate is any company that controls, is controlled by, or is under common control with, your company. This generally means that your affiliates are your parent company, your subsidiaries, and your sister companies. For example, if your organization is a bank owned by a bank holding company that also owns another bank, both the bank holding company and the other bank are your bank's affiliates.

To determine if you meet the asset size requirement, count only your assets. Do not count your affiliate's assets.

To determine if you meet the number of originations requirement, count all first-lien, closed-end mortgages made by you and made by your affiliates that are subject to the ATR requirements. Do not count subordinate-lien mortgages. Also do not count mortgages that are not subject to the ATR/QM rule, such as HELOCs, time-share plans, reverse mortgages, or temporary or bridge loans with terms of 12 months or less. (*See "What transactions are covered by the ATR/QM rule?"*)

### *i. Type 1: Small Creditor QM (§ 1026.43(e)(5))*

Small Creditor QM loans may not have negative-amortization, interest-only, or balloon-payment features or terms that exceed 30 years. They also may not have points and fees that exceed the specified QM limits. (*See "What are the QM points-and-fees caps and what do I include when calculating points and fees?"*)

In addition, in order for a loan to be a Small Creditor QM loan:

- You must underwrite based on a fully-amortizing schedule using the maximum rate permitted during the first five years after the date of the first periodic payment.
- The loan must not be subject to a forward commitment (an agreement made at or prior to consummation of a loan to sell the loan after consummation, other than to a creditor that itself is eligible to make Small Creditor QMs).
- You must consider and verify the consumer's income or assets, and debts, alimony, and child support.
- You must consider the consumer's debt-to-income ratio (DTI) or residual income, although the rule sets no specific threshold for DTI or residual income.

Small Creditor QMs generally lose their QM status if you sell or otherwise transfer them less than three years after consummation. However, a Small Creditor QM keeps its QM status if it meets one of these criteria:

- It is sold more than three years after consummation.
- It is sold to another creditor that meets the criteria regarding number of originations and asset size, at any time.
- It is sold pursuant to a supervisory action or agreement, at any time.
- It is transferred as part of a merger or acquisition of or by the creditor, at any time.

***ii. Type 2: Balloon-Payment QM (§ 1026.43(e)(6) and(f))***

The Bureau is providing a two-year transition period during which all small creditors can make Balloon-Payment QMs, regardless of where the small creditor operates. After that two-year period expires, only small creditors that operate predominantly in rural or underserved areas will be able to make Balloon-Payment QMs. **On or before** January 10, 2016 (two years after the effective date of the ATR/QM rule), you can originate Balloon-Payment QMs if you satisfy the asset size and number of originations requirements. Balloon-Payment QMs that are originated during this two-year period will retain their QM status after January 10, 2016, assuming the requirements to hold the loan in portfolio are met.

**After** January 10, 2016, you can originate Balloon- Payment QMs only if you meet the asset size and number of originations criteria as well as a requirement that you operate predominantly in rural or underserved areas.

**Balloon-Payment QMs** must not have negative- amortization or interest-only features and must comply with the points-and-fees limits for Qualified Mortgages.

In addition:

- The loan must have a fixed interest rate and periodic payments (other than the balloon payment) that would fully amortize the loan over 30 years or less.
- The loan must have a term of five years or longer.
- The loan must not be subject to a forward commitment (an agreement made at or prior to consummation of a loan to sell the loan after consummation, other than to a creditor that itself is eligible to make Balloon-Payment QMs).

**Implementation Tip:** After January 10, 2016, in order to make Balloon-Payment QMs, more than half of your organization's first-lien covered transactions during any of the three preceding calendar years must have been secured by properties in rural areas (equivalent to the USDA's Economic Research Service Urban Influence Codes 4, 6, 7, 8, 9, 10, 11, or 12) or underserved areas (counties where no more than two creditors extend five or more first-lien covered transactions in a calendar year). The Bureau will publish an annual list of rural or underserved counties. This is not the same definition of "rural" used for Home Mortgage Disclosure Act (HMDA) reporting or used by other agencies. For example, you may not be considered rural under this definition even though you are considered rural under HMDA and are not a HMDA reporter.

- You must determine that the consumer will be able to make the scheduled periodic payments (including mortgage-related obligations) other than the balloon payment. Unlike the calculation of balloon loan monthly payments for determining ATR (*See "Calculating payments under the ATR standard for the loan you are underwriting: § 1026.43(c)(5)"*), the Balloon-Payment QM calculation excludes the balloon payment even if the loan is a higher-priced loan,
- You must consider and verify the consumer's income or assets, and debts, alimony, and child support.
- You must consider the consumer's debt-to-income ratio (DTI) or residual income, although the rule sets no specific threshold for DTI or residual income.

Like Small Creditor QMs, Balloon-Payment QMs generally lose their QM status if you sell or otherwise transfer them less than three years after consummation. However, a Balloon-Payment QM keeps its QM status if it meets one of these criteria:

- It is sold more than three years after consummation.
- It is sold to another creditor that meets the criteria regarding operating in rural or underserved areas, number of originations, and asset size, at any time.
- It is sold pursuant to a supervisory action or agreement, at any time.
- It is transferred as part of a merger or acquisition of or by the creditor, at any time.

## VII. Are there Special Requirements for Calculating the DTI Ratio on QM loans? (§ 1026.43(e) (2)(vi) and Appendix Q)

As described above, the General QM definition requires that a consumer's total debt-to-income ratio not exceed 43 percent. Section 1026.43(e)(2)(vi) and appendix Q of the ATR/QM rule contain the definitions of debt and income for purposes of the General QM definition.

Keep in mind that different DTI rules apply to loans complying under the ATR standard and to the other QM definitions:

- To satisfy the general ATR standard, you must consider DTI or residual income.
- To originate a QM under the temporary definition (eligible for sale to or guarantee by a GSE or insured or guaranteed by a specified federal agency), you must meet the relevant entity's applicable DTI and other requirements.
- To originate a Small Creditor or Balloon-Payment QM, you must consider DTI or residual income, but you do not have to meet a specific threshold requirement.

## VIII. What Are the QM Points-and-Fees Caps and What Do I Include when Calculating Points and Fees? (§§ 1026.32(b) (1) and 1026.43(e)(3))

For a loan to be a QM, the points and fees may not exceed the points-and-fees caps. The points- and-fees caps are higher for smaller loans.

- 3 percent of the total loan amount for a loan greater than or equal to $100,000
- $3,000 for a loan greater than or equal to $60,000 but less than $100,000
- 5 percent of the total loan amount for a loan greater than or equal to $20,000 but less than $60,000
- $1,000 for a loan greater than or equal to $12,500 but less than $20,000
- 8 percent of the total loan amount for a loan less than $12,500

The dollar amounts listed above will be adjusted annually for inflation and published each year in the commentary to Regulation Z. *(See § 1026.43(e)(3)(ii) and accompanying Commentary.)*

**To determine whether a loan is within the QM points-and-fees caps, follow these steps:**

- First, determine which of the caps applies to the loan amount on the face of the note.
- Second, calculate the maximum points and fees for that loan amount:
- For a loan amount that has a **fixed-dollar cap** (for example, $3,000 for loan amounts of $60,000 but less than $100,000), that fixed-dollar cap is the maximum allowable points and fees.
- For a loan amount that has a **percentage cap** (for example, 5 percent of the total loan amount for loan amounts greater than or equal to $20,000 but less than $60,000) determine the "total loan amount" for your transaction. The total loan amount equals the "amount financed" (§ 1026.18) minus any points and fees that are rolled into the loan amount. Multiply the total loan amount by the percentage cap to determine the maximum allowable points and fees.
- Finally, calculate the total points and fees for your transaction. If the total points and fees for your transaction exceed the maximum allowable points and fees, then the loan cannot be a QM.

### *i. Points-and-fees calculation (§ 1026.32(b)(1))*

To calculate points and fees for the QM points-and-fees caps, you will use the same approach that you use for calculating points and fees for closed-end loans under the Home Ownership and Equity Protection Act (HOEPA) thresholds in the Bureau's High-Cost Mortgage and Homeownership Counseling Amendments to the Truth in Lending Act (Regulation Z) and Homeownership Counseling Amendments to the Real Estate Settlement Procedures Act (Regulation X) rulemakings. Those rules are available online at http://www.consumerfinance.gov/regulations/.

Unless specified otherwise, include amounts that are **known at or before consummation**, even if the consumer pays them after consummation by rolling them into the loan amount.

In addition, unless specified otherwise, closing costs that you pay and recoup from the consumer over time through the interest rate are not counted in points and fees.

To calculate points and fees, add together the amounts paid in connection with the transaction for the six categories of charges listed below:

### 1. Finance charge (§ 1026.32(b)(1)(i))

In general, include all items included in the finance charge. (§ 1026.4(a) and (b)). However, you may **exclude** the following types and amounts of charges, even if they normally would be included in the finance charge:

- Interest or the time-price differential
- Mortgage insurance premiums (MIPs)
- Federal or state government-sponsored MIPs: For example, exclude up-front and annual FHA premiums, VA funding fees, and USDA guarantee fees.
- Private mortgage insurance (PMI) premiums: Exclude monthly or annual PMI premiums. You may also exclude up-front PMI premiums if the premium is refundable on a prorated basis and a refund is automatically issued upon loan satisfaction. However, even if the premium is excludable, you must include any portion that exceeds the up- front MIP for FHA loans. Those amounts are published in HUD Mortgagee Letters, which you can access on HUD's website at http://portal.hud.gov/hudportal/HUD?src=/program_offices/administration/hudclips/letters/mortgagee/.
- A charge paid by a third party may be included in points and fees, but is not included in points and fees under § 1026.32(b)(1)(i) if the exclusions to points and fees in § 1026.32(b)(1)(i)(A) through (F) apply. For example, seller's points are not included in points and fees under § 1026.32(b)(1)(i) as they are not included in the finance charge. But they still may be included in points and fees under § 1026.32(b)(1)(ii) through (vi) – for example, if they cover loan originator compensation, credit life insurance premiums, or a prepayment penalty.
- *Bona fide* third-party charges not retained by the creditor, loan originator, or an affiliate of either (§ 1026.32(b)(1)(i)(D))
- In general, you may exclude these types of charges even if they would be included in the finance charge. For example, you may exclude a *bona fide* charge imposed by a third-party settlement agent (for example, an attorney) so long as neither the creditor nor the loan originator (or their affiliates) retains a portion of the charge.
- However, you must still **include** any third-party charges that are specifically required to be included under other provisions of the points-and-fees calculation (for example, certain PMI premiums, certain real estate-related charges, and premiums for certain credit insurance and debt cancellation or suspension coverage). Note that up-front fees you charge consumers to recover the costs of loan-level price adjustments imposed by secondary market purchasers of loans, including the GSEs, are not considered *bona fide* third-party charges and must be included in points and fees.

- *Bona fide* discount points (§ 1026.32(b)(1)(i)(E), 32(b)(1)(i)(F), and 32(b)(3))
- Exclude up to 2 bona fide discount points if the interest rate before the discount does not exceed the APOR for a comparable transaction by more than 1 percentage point; or
- Exclude up to 1 *bona fide* discount point if the interest rate before the discount does not exceed the APOR for a comparable transaction by more than 2 percentage points.

Note that a discount point is "bona fide" if it reduces the consumer's interest rate by an amount that reflects established industry practices, such as secondary mortgage market norms. An example is the pricing in the to-be-announced market for mortgage-backed securities.

**2. Loan originator compensation (§ 1026.32(b)(1)(ii))**

Include compensation paid directly or indirectly by a consumer or creditor to a loan originator other than compensation paid by a mortgage broker, creditor, or retailer of manufactured homes to an employee. Include compensation that is attributable to the transaction, to the extent that such compensation is known as of the date the interest rate for the transaction is set. In general, include the following:

- **Compensation paid directly by a consumer to a mortgage broker:** Include the amount the consumer pays directly to the mortgage broker. If this payment is already included in points and fees because it is included in the finance charge under § 1026.32(b)(1)(i), it does not have to be included again as loan originator compensation under § 1026.32(b)(1)(ii).
- **Compensation paid by a creditor to a mortgage broker:** Include the amount the creditor pays to the broker for the transaction. Include this amount even if the creditor included origination or other charges paid by the consumer to the creditor as points and fees under § 1026.32(b)(1)(i) as a finance charge or if the creditor does not receive an up-front payment from the consumer to cover the broker's fee but rather recoups the fee from the consumer through the interest rate over time.
- **Compensation paid by a consumer or creditor to a manufactured home retailer:** Include the amount paid by a consumer or creditor to a manufactured home retailer that qualifies as a loan originator under

§ 1026.36(a)(1) for loan origination activities. Compensation paid by the manufactured home retailer to its employees does not have to be included. § 1026.32(b)(1)(ii)(D) and comment 32 (b)(1)(ii)-5.

- **Compensation included in the sales price of a manufactured home:** Include loan originator compensation that the creditor has knowledge that loan originator compensation is included in the sales price of a manufactured home. The creditor is not required to investigate the sales price of a manufactured home to determine if the sales price includes loan originator compensation. Comment 32(b)(1)(ii)-5.

**Implementation Tip**: In the context of determining what loan origination compensation must be included in points and fees, the term "mortgage broker" refers to both brokerage firms and individual brokers. Compensation paid by a mortgage broker to an employee is not included in points and fees.

### 3. Real estate-related fees (§ 1026.32(b)(1)(iii))

The following categories of charges are **excluded** from points and fees **only if:**

1. The charge is reasonable;
2. The creditor receives no direct or indirect compensation in connection with the charge; and
3. The charge is not paid to an affiliate of the creditor.

If one or more of those three conditions is **not** satisfied, **you must include** these charges in points and fees even if they would be excluded from the finance charge:

- Fees for title examination, abstract of title, title insurance, property survey, and similar purposes
- Fees for preparing loan-related documents, such as deeds, mortgages, and reconveyance or settlement documents
- Notary and credit-report fees
- Property appraisal fees or inspection fees to assess the value or condition of the property if the service is performed prior to consummation, including fees related to pest-infestation or flood-hazard determinations

- Amounts paid into escrow or trustee accounts that are not otherwise included in the finance charge (except amounts held for future payment of taxes)

**4. Premiums for credit insurance; credit property insurance; other life, accident, health or loss-of-income insurance where the creditor is beneficiary; or debt cancellation or suspension coverage payments (§ 1026.32(b)(1)(iv))**

Include premiums for these types of insurance that are payable at or before consummation even if such premiums are rolled into the loan amount, if permitted by law.

You do not need to include these charges if they are paid after consummation (e.g., monthly premiums).

Note that credit property insurance means insurance that protects the creditor's interest in the property. It does not include homeowner's insurance that protects the consumer.

You do not need to include premiums for life, accident, health, or loss-of-income insurance if the consumer (or another person designated by the consumer) is the sole beneficiary of the insurance.

**5. Maximum prepayment penalty (§ 1026.32(b)(1)(v))**

Include the maximum prepayment penalty that a consumer could be charged for prepaying the loan. To determine if you are permitted to charge a prepayment penalty, see "Can I charge prepayment fees on a covered transaction?" below.

**6. Prepayment penalty paid in a refinance (§ 1026.32(b)(1)(vi))**

If you are refinancing a loan that you or your affiliate currently holds or is currently servicing, then include any penalties you charge consumers for prepaying their previous loans.

**7. Charges paid by third parties. (Comment 32(b)(1)-2))**

Include charges paid by third parties that fall within the definition of points and fees in § 1026.32(b)(1)(i) through (vi) (discussed above), including charges included in the finance charge. Charges paid by third parties that fall within the exclusions to points and fees in § 1026.32(b)(1)(i)(A) through (F) do not have to be included in points and fees. Seller's points are excluded from the finance charge (see § 1026.4(c)(5)) and therefore can be excluded from points and fees, but charges paid by the seller should be included if they are for items listed as points and fees in § 1026.32(b)(1)(ii) through (vi).

**8. Creditor-paid charges. (Comment 32(b)(1)-2))**

Charges paid by the creditor, other than loan originator compensation paid by the creditor that is required to be included in points and fees under § 1026.32(b)(1)(ii), can be excluded from points and fees.

## IX. Can I Charge Prepayment Fees on a Covered Transaction? (§ 1026.43(g))

If you wish to include a prepayment penalty option, you may only do so for fixed-rate or step- rate QMs that are not higher-priced and only when applicable law otherwise permits the prepayment penalty.

Note that the definition of prepayment penalty does not include certain bona fide third-party charges that were waived at consummation (and expected to be reimbursed via the interest rate) in cases where the consumer fully prepays the loan within three years and must repay the charges.

Include the maximum prepayment penalty amount when you calculate the loan's fees and points to determine whether the points and fees exceed the limits discussed above. *(See "What are the QM points-and-fees caps and what do I include when calculating points and fees?")*

You cannot impose a prepayment penalty after the first three years of the loan term.

A prepayment penalty also **cannot** be greater than:

- 2 percent of the outstanding loan balance prepaid during the first two years of the loan
- 1 percent of the outstanding loan balance prepaid during the third year of the loan

If you wish to charge a prepayment fee, **you must also offer the consumer an alternative transaction that you believe the consumer will qualify for. The alternative loan cannot have** a prepayment penalty. The alternative loan must be similar to the loan with the prepayment penalty, so the consumer can choose between two products he will likely qualify for.

The **alternative loan**:

- Must be a fixed-rate or graduated-payment loan and must match the rate type from the loan with the prepayment penalty
- Must have the same term as the mortgage with the prepayment penalty
- Cannot have deferred principal, balloon or interest-only payments, or negative amortization

When your organization is a broker or table-funds loans and you want to use the safe harbor for compliance with anti-steering rules for loan originators under § 1026.36(e) of Regulation Z, you must show the consumer:

- The loan with the lowest interest rate overall
- The loan with the lowest interest rate with a prepayment penalty
- The loan with the lowest total origination points or fee and discount points

**Implementation Tip:** The alternative loans do not have to come from the same secondary market partner. You may show the consumer alternative loans from more than one investor or aggregator.

## 5. Refinancing from Non-Standard to Standard Loans: ATR Special Circumstance (§ 1026.43(D))

### I. Do the Standard ATR Requirements Apply when I Refinance Consumers from a Non-Standard to a Standard Loan? (§ 1026.43(d)(1)(ii)(A))

Many consumers have adjustable-rate, interest-only, or negative-amortization loans that they may not be able to afford when the loan recasts. To give you more flexibility to help these homeowners refinance, the ATR/QM rule gives you the option to **refinance your current mortgage customers** from a **non-standard** mortgage (which includes various types of mortgages that can lead to payment shock and can result in default) into a **standard mortgage** without having to meet the rule's ATR requirements including considering the eight underwriting factors required for ATR.

This option applies only to mortgages your organization holds or services. Subservicers and third parties cannot use it.

You can use this option **only** when:

- The payments under the refinance will not cause the consumer's principal balance to increase.
- The consumer uses the proceeds to pay off the original mortgage and for closing or settlement charges appearing on the HUD-1 settlement statement. The consumer takes out no cash.
- The consumer's monthly payment will materially decrease (*i.e.*, at least 10 percent).
- The consumer has only one 30-day late payment in the past 12 months and no late payments within six months.
- The consumer's written application for the standard mortgage is received no later than two months after the non-standard mortgage has recast.
- You have considered whether the standard mortgage likely will prevent the consumer from defaulting on the non-standard mortgage once the loan is recast.
- If the non-standard mortgage was consummated on or after January 10, 2014, the non- standard mortgage was made in accordance with the rule's Ability-to-Repay requirements or Qualified Mortgage provisions, as applicable.

The new loan has to meet these guidelines:

- The loan cannot have deferred principal, negative amortization, or balloon payments.
- Points and fees must fall within the thresholds for Qualified Mortgages.
- The loan term cannot exceed 40 years.
- The interest rate must be fixed for at least the first five years of the loan.

**Implementation Tip:** The ATR/QM rule does not apply when you alter an existing loan without refinancing it. So you can provide a loan modification to a defaulted (or non-defaulted) consumer without complying with ATR. You can find a discussion of what changes to a loan will be treated as a modification rather than a refinancing in Regulation Z at § 1026.20(a).

### II. How Do I Calculate Non-Standard and Standard Payment Amounts to Determine Whether the Consumer's Monthly Payment on the Standard Mortgage will Represent a Material Decrease? (§ 1026.43(d)(5))

To calculate payments when comparing non-standard loans to standard loans, first calculate the payment the consumer will have to make if the non-standard loan reaches a recast point. **Recast** occurs when:

- For an adjustable-rate mortgage, the introductory fixed-rate period ends.
- For an interest-only loan, the interest-only period ends.
- For a negatively-amortizing loan, the negatively-amortizing payment period ends.

Then calculate the payment for the standard loan, using the fully-indexed rate and the monthly payment that will fully amortize the loan based on equal monthly payments.

Finally, compare the two payments. A material decrease must be evaluated in light of the facts and circumstances for the particular loan. A payment reduction of 10 percent or more meets the "materially lower" standard.

Note that the payment calculation for this special refinancing provision is slightly different from the payment calculation used under the ATR/QM provisions. Under this special provision, you must base the calculation of the maximum loan amount on the amount of principal that will be outstanding at the time of recast, taking into account any principal payments that the consumer will have made by that time.

## 6. Practical Implementation and Compliance Considerations

You should consult with legal counsel or your compliance officer to understand your obligations under the rule, and to devise the policies and procedures you will need to have in place to comply with the rule's requirements.

How you comply with the rule may depend on your business model. When mapping out your compliance plan, you should consider practical implementation issues in addition to understanding your obligations under the rule. Your compliance plan may include:

1. **Identifying affected products, departments, and staff**
   Creditors may offer some, or all, of the loan products discussed in the ATR/QM rule. To plan for implementation of the rule, you should identify all products, departments, and staff affected by the rule.
2. **Identifying the business-process, operational, and technology changes that will be necessary for compliance**
   The new requirements may affect a number of parts of your business systems and processes. The forms and processes you use to communicate internally and externally may be affected by the verification requirements. The systems and processes you use to underwrite loans may also be affected. Secondary marketing and servicing processes and systems may be affected by the special ATR provisions regarding the refinancing of a non-standard loan into a standard loan. It is likely that as you originate new loans after January 10, 2014, you will want to identify those loans on your transaction systems with their definitional status under the rule (i.e., ATR, QM), which may involve creating new data element(s) within your processing systems. Likewise, if the loan is a QM, you probably want to note which level of liability protection the loan is receiving, which may have similar impacts.
   Fully understanding the changes required may involve a review of your existing business processes, as well as the hardware and software that you, your agents, or other business partners use. Gap analyses may be a helpful output of such a review and help you to create a robust implementation plan.
3. **Identifying critical impacts on key service providers or business partners**
   Third-party updates may be necessary to obtain required information or verifications, update disclosures, underwriting software, compliance and quality-control systems and processes; and update records-management protocols.
   Software providers, or other vendors and business partners, may offer compliance solutions that can assist with any necessary changes.

Identifying these key partners will depend on your business model. For example, banks and credit unions may find it helpful to talk to their correspondent banks, secondary market partners, and technology vendors. In some cases, you may need to negotiate revised or new contracts with these parties, or seek a different set of services.

If you seek the assistance of vendors or business partners, make sure you understand the extent of the assistance that they provide. For example, if vendors provide software that calculates loan cost to determine which transactions are higher-priced, do they guarantee the accuracy of their conclusions?

The CFPB expects supervised banks and nonbanks to have an effective process for managing the risks of scrvicc provider relationships. For more information on this, view CFPB Bulletin 2012-03 Service Providers.

4. **Identifying training needs**

   Consider what training will be necessary for your loan officers; secondary marketing, processing, compliance, and-quality control staff; as well as anyone else who approves, processes, or monitors credit transactions. Training may also be necessary for other individuals who are your employees, or for the employees of your agents and business partners.

5. **Considering other Title XIV rules**

   The ATR/QM rule is just one component of the Bureau's Dodd-Frank Act Title XIV rulemakings.

   Other Title XIV rules include:

   - 2013 HOEPA Rule
   - ECOA Valuations Rule
   - TILA Higher-Priced Mortgage Loans Appraisal Rule
   - Loan Originator Rule
   - RESPA and TILA Mortgage Servicing Rules
   - TILA Higher-Priced Mortgage Loans Escrow Rule

Each of these rules affects aspects of the mortgage industry and its regulation. Many of these rules intersect with one or more of the others. Therefore, the compliance considerations for these rules may overlap in your organization. You will find copies of these rules online at http://www.consumerfinance.gov/regulations/.

# 7. OTHER RESOURCES

## I. Where Can I Find a Copy of the ATR/QM Rule and Get More Information about It?

You will find the January 2013 Final Rule on the Bureau's website at http://www.consumerfinance.gov/regulations/Ability-To-Repay-and-qualified-mortgage-standards-under-the-truth-in-lending-act-regulation-z/.

In addition to a complete copy of the January 2013 Final Rule, that web page also contains:

- The preamble, which explains why the Bureau issued the rule; the legal authority and reasoning behind the rule; responses to comments; and analysis of the benefits, costs, and impacts of the rule
- Official Interpretations of the rule
- Links to final rule amendments, including the June 2013 ATR/QM Concurrent Final Rule, the July 2013 Final Rule, and the October 2013 Final Rule
- Other implementation support materials including videos, reference charts, and proposed rule amendments

Useful resources related to regulatory implementation are also available at http://www.consumerfinance.gov/regulatory-implementation/.

For email updates about Bureau regulations and when additional Dodd-Frank Act Title XIV implementation resources become available, please submit your email address within the "Email updates about mortgage rule implementation" box at http://www.consumerfinance.gov/regulatory-implementation/.

# INDEX

## G



## H



## I



## J



## L

## M



## N



## O



## P



## Q



## R

## S



## T



## U



## V

## W